7 Ways of Teaching the Bible to Children

Barbara Bruce

Abingdon Press
Nashville

7 Ways of Teaching the Bible to Children

Copyright © 1996 by Abingdon Press

This book is printed on acid-free, recycled paper.

Scripture quotations, unless otherwise noted, are from the New Revised Standard Version of the Bible, copyright © 1989 by the Division of Christian Education of the National Council of the Churches of Christ in the USA.

Those noted NIV are from the *Holy Bible, New International Version*. Copyright © 1973, 1978, 1984 International Bible Society. Used by permission of Zondervan Publishing House. All rights reserved.

Library of Congress Cataloging-in-Publication Data

Bruce, Barbara.
    7 ways of teaching the Bible to children / Barbara Bruce.
      p. cm.
    Includes bibliographical references and index.
    ISBN 0-687-02068-9 (pbk. : alk. paper)
    1. Bible—Study and teaching.   2. Christian education of children.   3. Cognitive styles in children.
I. Title.
BS600.2.B76   1996
268'.432—dc20   96-42570
                                                                 CIP

Permission to reproduce pages 75-77 and pages 95-110 is granted to purchasers of this book.

99   00   01   02   03   04   05 — 10   9   8   7   6   5   4   3

MANUFACTURED IN THE UNITED STATES OF AMERICA

To my daughter
Stacey,
who flourishes in spite of the system
and who learns in many ways.
For Stacey and all children
who learn in different ways,
there is hope.

CONTENTS

TRAINING WORKSHOP

APPENDIX

BIBLIOGRAPHY

FOREWORD

From the very beginning, the Wesleyan movement touted a singular formula: knowledge + vital piety = an awakened church. Education is the key to spiritual awakening. It is often forgotten that Wesley himself was a formidable Oxford don, doughty to the point where he supposedly refused to enter the university town of Cambridge, England, because he did not want to lower his academic standards.

The Methodist movement was born in a learning setting (Oxford University). It will be born again in learning settings as well (what I call "church seminaries"). In fact, education may be more central to a spiritual awakening than worship. Wesley stressed substantive teaching and preaching over recruiting new members. After all, he called his meetings "classes." The early Wesleyans were more concerned about how to send people out rather than seduce them in.

If our churches were sending out educated disciples, our churches wouldn't have to worry so much about bringing in new people to worship. Instead of peopling buildings, we would be building people. Instead of making programs, we would be making disciples.

One of the best resources I have encountered that uses new learning theory and creativity studies to teach the stories of the faith is Barbara Bruce's interactive, experiential work/playbook, *7 Ways of Teaching the Bible to Children*. Full disclosure? I confess: this book deepened and widened my own understanding of the biblical texts (which says more about the value of this book than the state of my faith, I hope).

Do something "unadultish." Use this book not just as an educational resource for children, but also for your own spiritual enjoyment, enrichment, and instruction. Bruce wrote the book for children—which means she wrote it for all of us.

Leonard Sweet
Drew University

INTRODUCTION

Multiple Intelligence Theory

In 1984 a group of cutting-edge educators left a conference in Tarrytown, New York, energized and excited about a presentation that was to change the shape of teaching across the country. Like a pebble tossed into a pond, the ripple effect of that presentation is reaching into school systems and touching children's lives.

The presenter's name was Howard Gardner. At the time he was refining his theory of multiple intelligences, which he developed during his graduate work at Harvard University. Later his findings were published in a book titled *Frames of Mind: The Theory of Multiple Intelligences*. Gardner's theory, simply stated, is that cognitive learning takes many forms in the human brain. Each of us is born with the capacity to "learn" in many different ways. However, each of us develops preferred ways of learning, and we rely most heavily on those ways to learn.

Gardner isolated seven intelligences, but maintains that these seven intelligences seldom stand alone. They are integrated into patterns of our own selecting, which provide us with our best means of gathering knowledge. Gardner's work is not finished, and is a beginning, rather than an end. He and others, like David Lazear, are continually searching for other patterns and ways of knowing.

When educators limit their teaching to a few of the many ways that persons learn, as is most common in Western culture, they are depriving some children of their most preferred ways of learning. Limiting the methods of teaching forces all children to learn in the ways that are preferred only by some children or by the teacher.

As Christian teachers we can provide extended ways for children to learn the stories that form and shape our faith. By including all of the seven intelligences in our teaching on a regular basis, we are:

- ensuring that *every* child will learn in her or his preferred way
- enriching our lessons by using many and varied techniques
- encouraging new learning to take place
- extending our ability to spread God's Word

GARDNER'S SEVEN INTELLIGENCES

VERBAL/LINGUISTIC:	The use of the spoken and written word in learning.
LOGICAL/MATHEMATICAL:	The use of abstract patterns and concepts, numbers, linear and sequential thinking.
VISUAL/SPATIAL:	The use of physically seeing and mentally picturing images as a way of learning.
BODY/KINESTHETIC:	The use of our bodies as a means of learning.
MUSICAL/RHYTHMIC:	The use of sounds, rhythms, tunes, and songs in learning.
INTERPERSONAL:	The use of communicating with one or more persons to share learnings.
INTRAPERSONAL:	The use of inner knowledge and reflection as a means of learning.

Now that we have a brief description of this information, what shall we do with it? Please read on.

In this book you will find:

✓ an overview of each intelligence and general suggestions for their use

✓ warm-up activities to spark learning in a particular intelligence

✓ twenty-five lessons on familiar biblical stories that can easily be used independently, or as companions to your regular curriculum

✓ examples that provide a format for a culminating lesson, a culminating activity session, groups of lessons that build on one another, several single-focus lessons to give you many and varied lesson teaching options

✓ lessons focused on one intelligence with three additional intelligences integrated into each lesson for more comprehensive learning, along with suggested activities involving the remaining intelligences to give *every* child an opportunity to learn at her or his optimum level

✔ a spark to start your own creative fires burning

✔ a reproducible worksheet for adapting each plan to your specific situation, with space for recording your ideas for using other intelligences, and your reactions to the lesson

✔ a teacher training session and handout for participants

✔ samples of patterns and activities for use with the various lessons

✔ a bibliography for expanding your knowledge

Enjoy this book. Use it. Experiment with it. Try your own ideas. God bless.

Scriptural References to Multiple Intelligences

The Bible is filled with references to the use of all seven intelligences. Included here is a partial (*) listing to demonstrate that learning through the use of various intelligences is *not* something new, the latest fad, or unique to Western culture.

The Bible cites numerous examples of each intelligence and how it was a part of the total story of our relationship with God.

VERBAL/LINGUISTIC

Old Testament: Genesis 13:14-18	God speaks to Abram
New Testament: Matthew 5:1-12	Jesus' Sermon on the Mount

LOGICAL/MATHEMATICAL

Old Testament: Exodus 20:1-17	The Ten Commandments
New Testament: Romans 5:1-5	Summary of Paul's view of the cause and effect of faith

VISUAL/SPATIAL

Old Testament: Isaiah 11:6-9	Images of the peaceable kingdom
New Testament: Matthew 13:1-9	The parable of the sower

BODY/KINESTHETIC

Old Testament: Exodus 14:21-25   Moses and the Israelites cross
the Red Sea

New Testament: Mark 2:3-12   The healing of the paralyzed man

MUSICAL/RHYTHMIC

Old Testament: Psalm 47   God rules over the nations

Exodus 15   The song of Moses

New Testament: Colossians 3:16   Sing psalms and hymns to God

INTERPERSONAL

Old Testament: Esther 4:9-17   Esther and Mordecai plan together

New Testament: Luke 9:1-6   The mission of the Twelve

INTRAPERSONAL

Old Testament: Psalm 22:1-11   Suffering and praise

New Testament: Luke 22:39-42   Jesus prays alone at Gethsemane

*You might want to come up with your own list of scriptural accounts of these intelligences.

Determining Children's Preferences

We are created in God's image, yet each of us is a unique and special creation. We are born with the capacity to learn through all seven intelligences, yet each of us is put together with preferences in a unique combination. To tap into the God-given uniqueness of each child, we must recognize and utilize *all* the intelligences as we teach, to ensure that each child is learning at her or his peak capacity. To limit our teaching/learning styles to one or two of the intelligences is to place our limits on God's creativity.

Your Sunday school classroom is filled with unique children of God. Their learning preferences vary and form individual configurations. As teachers we tend to "teach" in the ways we are most comfortable. For those who learn in the same patterns as we do, that is just fine. When we use these teaching patterns with children who are put together with different learning preferences, we will produce bored, unimaginative, and inattentive students. Discipline problems bubble up quickly when we do not tap into a student's preferred ways of learning.

The following clues will help you identify intelligence preferences. The child who prefers:

VERBAL/LINGUISTIC learning will enjoy using language in all forms—both spoken and written. Given a choice this child will read or write. Words are tools to be used in learning. This child becomes frustrated without verbal stimulation and challenging concepts.

LOGICAL/MATHEMATICAL learning loves abstract thinking, is logical and precise, enjoys figuring out solutions to problems. Given a choice this child will use a calculator or computer. Rational thinking is a tool to be used in learning. This child finds it difficult to function in arenas of confusion or chaos, too much repetition, and unspecified goals.

VISUAL/SPATIAL learning sees information in terms of colors and pictures. Given a choice this child will draw or map out a concept for clarity. Given a choice this child will find pictures, maps, illustrations to "see" the concept. Pictures are tools to enhance learning. Too much printed material and too much writing will frustrate and discourage learning.

BODY/KINESTHETIC learning acquires information through movement and manipulating objects. Given a choice this child will walk through a concept and find physical objects to identify with. Opportunities to move and objects to manipulate provide this child with a successful learning experience. Too much sitting and inactivity for too long will cause this child to tune out.

MUSICAL/RHYTHMIC learning loves to tap out a beat when thinking. They learn best when surrounded by sound and will enjoy playing with rhythms. Given a choice this child chooses music in any form for the best learning. Beat and rhythm are learning tools. This child is bored with long reading or writing assignments. Long lectures and large amounts of seat work cause stress.

INTERPERSONAL learning functions best on a team. Motivation and learning stem from cooperative learning tasks and bouncing ideas off others. Given a choice this child will work with others on a project or shared study. Cooperative or paired learning is how this child flourishes. This child is stifled by introspection, and long periods of silent study.

13

INTRAPERSONAL learning loves private time to think and evaluate information. Given a choice this child selects journaling and introspection. Reflection and self-determined learning paths are motivating. This child is uncomfortable with teacher-directed activities that appear without reason, direct instruction, and generalities.

3 Ways to Identify Intelligence Preferences

1. Set up seven learning centers, one devoted to each individual intelligence. Explain each center in terms of the activities associated with a particular intelligence (e.g., writing, drawing, pretending to be one of the animals on Noah's ark, and so on), and allow the students to "self-select." Through careful observation you will be able to identify which students gravitate to which activities.

2. For younger children use the "Identifying Intelligence Preference" form on page 97. Place one sheet in each learning center. Encourage the children to visit each center and mark a sad or happy face for the activity beside their name.

3. For older children, follow the same procedure as in no. 2, but ask them to write a comment about each activity in stub sentences (page 18).

How to Use These Bible Lessons

✓ Each lesson features a scripture reference. Read the story to older children or invite them to read it aloud. For younger children read from a children's Bible or tell the story in age-appropriate language. The important thing is that your students understand the message from the Bible and reinforce it with the rest of the lesson.

✓ Each lesson identifies a focus or main idea that is learned from the lesson. The lesson activities work to present that focus in a particular intelligence to ensure optimum learning for the children.

✓ Each lesson features a primary intelligence that is supported by and intertwined with several other intelligences.

✓ Each lesson lists the materials needed for the lesson. If you decide to include other intelligences in the lesson, make sure you have the materials you will need on hand.

✓ Each lesson suggests a setting for the activities. If your classroom does not allow for this kind of space, move to a hallway, fellowship area, or outdoors. An activity can be modified to suit your teaching space, or simply choose one of the Variations, which are included in each lesson.

✓ Each lesson explains the learning process that is used to incorporate various intelligences into the lesson.

✓ Each lesson includes a warm-up activity. These activities are very important to prime students' minds to the primary intelligence of the lesson, before actually getting into the content of the lesson. This is a time for students to practice and experience the featured intelligence. This is also a time for students to move into a learning mode and to have fun.

✓ Each lesson then works through the learnings and activities in large or small group settings. Time constraints may not allow you to incorporate all seven of the intelligences into each lesson. Select the activities that fit your students' learning needs, and add at least one activity that will stretch their comfort level and their thinking. To help facilitate teaching/learning, there are activities suggested for younger children (ages 5-8) and older children (ages 9-11). These activities are age-level appropriate. They are also flexible enough to be altered to your specific student needs.

Establishing learning centers assists children in learning the Bible. Not every center needs to be used every week, but by providing several centers (based on suggestions in the lesson) you can expand teaching/learning capacity. Providing choices may help to cut down on discipline problems as children are occupied with ways of learning that suit them best. Here are several ideas for centers:

- a small, quiet place for intrapersonal activities
- a place that can be sectioned off with tape players and musical possibilities
- an area for movement and role play (perhaps with simple costumes and props)
- an area for thinking and figuring out puzzles and mind games
- a table for reading and writing
- an area of your room that is visually stimulating with pictures/maps/bulletin board
- an area where students can work in small groups

Your room does not have to be large to include all of these centers, it just takes some creative thinking and good use of space.

✓ Each lesson suggests ways of using the activities that the children complete. Busywork is just that, and students become turned off by doing activities that have little or no relevance to the lesson or to them.

15

✓ Each lesson lists Variations that include suggestions for other intelligences. These ideas are handy if you want to substitute activities that are different from those presented in the lesson, or they can be added to the learning centers for the optimum use of time and space for learning.

✓ At the end of each lesson record your ideas, suggestions, and other possibilities for teaching/learning on the form provided on page 98.

Learning Activities Descriptions

Acrostic: A composition in which the first letters of each line form a name or a title and each line describes the object named.

EX:

```
J  oy of my heart
E  mmanuel
S  avior
U  niversal Lord
S  eeking me
```

Continuum: A line depicting both extremes of any thought. Persons can select their belief any place from one end of the continuum to the other.

EX: right to life _____ free choice

Diorama: A box that contains a three-dimensional picture starting with background scenery on the back of the box and objects relating to the picture glued in the foreground.

Echo-pantomime: A series of short phrases with movements to depict the words. A leader says the words and performs the motions, the audience repeats both the words and motions one phrase at a time.

EX: Come, follow me. (Extend hand and bring it toward you.)

Journal Entries: A journal depicts a day in the life of a particular person describing their feelings and reactions to events that occurred that day.

Concept Map: A visual representation of a word, idea, or concept and all the thoughts that surround it. One thought usually spurs another and another. Often thoughts are linked by lines to show connections. (See example on page 102.)

Rebus: A representation of a name, word, or phrase by pictures.

EX: A man caught a large fish.

Role Play: An acting out of a story without the use of a written script. The characters behave in the way they believe their character would in the story being told.

Sequencing Cards: A set of cards (pictures for young children/phrases for older children) that recreate a story in the order that it happened.

EX:

Stabile: A stationary form that displays pictures or drawings that are attached to it and do not move.

Stub Sentences: The first few words of a sentence that invite a completion of the sentence by a person adding some thoughts or feelings.

EX: I am sad when _____ .

T-Chart: A chart divided in half to resemble the letter *T* on which persons record what they see on one side of the center line and what they hear on the other side. (See page 103.)

Venn Diagram: A diagram used as a visual way to depict differences and similarities. It is comprised of two or three circles that have a space uniquely theirs and a space that interconnects the circles. Differences between things are recorded in the space that is uniquely separate and similarities are recorded in the space that interconnects. (See page 100.)

Walk a Pattern: A Body/Kinesthetic way of learning by repeating words or phrases as persons walk in a specific pattern. The mind and body connect the learnings and eventually the words or phrases can be repeated just by walking the pattern.

What? So What? Now What? Chart: A chart to provide a visual picture of learning through cause and effect. What? refers to the information learned. So What? refers to placing this information in the context of other learning and relating it to me. Now What? refers to how this information will change my actions or how I am going to use this learning.

EX:

What?	So What?	Now What?
Jews and Samaritans were enemies.	For a Samaritan to help a Jew who had been hurt was a big challenge.	Jesus tells me to be kind to all people, even my enemies.

LESSON 1

GOD'S CREATION

 **SCRIPTURE** Genesis 1:1–2:4

 **LESSON FOCUS** God was the Creator
of all the world.

 **INTELLIGENCE FOCUS** VISUAL/SPATIAL
Interpersonal
Verbal/Linguistic

 **MATERIALS**

- [ ] children's Bible
- [ ] several sheets of light
  colored paper
- [ ] pencils
- [ ] scissors
- [ ] light blue cloth cut and
  edged to fit altar
- [ ] fabric glue

 **LEARNING AREA**

- [ ] space where children can
  sit in pairs
- [ ] several large areas where
  children can draw, cut, and paste

 **LEARNING PROCESS** VISUAL/SPATIAL learning connects
with VERBAL/LINGUISTIC learning as
children listen to the creation story and
"see" it in their imaginations. VISUAL/SPATIAL and INTERPERSONAL learning connect with VERBAL/LINGUISTIC learning as students share their images with their group, create a group image in their small groups, and describe their image to the entire class as they interpret what they see using felt pieces to make a "Creation" altar cloth or banner.

 **WARM-UP**

VISUAL/SPATIAL learning: Invite the children to find a partner and sit side by side. Have them close their eyes and imagine a warm, sunny day. Ask them to imagine themselves walking along a path in a beautiful wooded area with flowers and trees all around them. The sun is shining through the trees and they can hear birds chirping as they walk along the path. Ask them to stop and pick up something from the path in front of them. Ask them to slowly open their eyes and blink three times.

Allow the children to take turns and tell one another what their "woods" looked like. What kinds of things did they see? What did they find on the path? What color was it? Encourage vivid descriptions.

Ask the children how this experience felt. Were they comfortable? Were they able to "see" things? Did they see in color?

 **LESSON**

Explain to the children that you are going to read them a story about how God made the world. Ask them to listen carefully as the story is read, and to picture what they are hearing in their minds. Read the creation story slowly and with emphasis from a descriptive children's Bible. Allow the children time to create visual images of the story.

When you have finished reading, ask the children to again talk with their partner about what they saw. On a chalkboard or a piece of newsprint draw a "T-Chart" (see page 103) to record what the children saw or heard on each day of the creation story.

Divide the class into seven groups. Have each group select a day of the week, and make paper patterns of the things that were created on that day. Trace the patterns onto pieces of felt. Cut out each felt design. Invite each group, beginning with day 1, to glue their images onto the blue background cloth. As they work have them tell the story of what God created on their particular day. Decide if this creation will become an altar cloth for your church or a banner for your classroom or hallway. Finish the edges of the cloth according to its use.

 **VARIATIONS**

Logical/Mathematical: Have students determine how the sequence that God chose built upon each day's creation. Ask them to create a chart of the daily creations.

Musical/Rhythmic: Have the students finish the rhythmic patterned story of creation that begins:

> On the first day, *clap, clap, clap,* God created, *clap, clap, clap,* light, day and night and God said, "It is good."

On the second day, *clap, clap, clap*, God created, *clap, clap, clap*, a dome called sky and God said, "It is good."

On the third day, *clap, clap, clap*, God created, *clap, clap, clap*, earth and sea and all the plants and God said, "It is good."

On the fourth day, *clap, clap, clap*, God created, *clap, clap, clap*. . . .

Body/Kinesthetic: Have children act out God's creation for each day. Ask them to become light, day and night, sky, earth and sea, and so on.

Intrapersonal: Ask the students to think about what they might have advised God to add to or subtract from each of the days of creation.

 **LESSON EVALUATION** See form on page 98.

21

LESSON 2

NOAH AND THE GREAT FLOOD

 **SCRIPTURE**   Genesis 6:1–7:4

 **LESSON FOCUS**   God saves the world through Noah, his family, and all God's creatures.

 **INTELLIGENCE FOCUS**   VISUAL/SPATIAL
Body/Kinesthetic
Logical/Mathematical
Verbal/Linguistic

 **MATERIALS**

- [ ] several sets of "sequence" pictures (three pictures of a sequence that can be photocopied)
- [ ] large sheets of paper (the backs of supermarket bags work well)
- [ ] markers

 **LEARNING AREA**

- [ ] table space for children to draw large pictures
- [ ] large floor space for children to walk through the story

 **LEARNING PROCESS**

VISUAL/SPATIAL learning connects with **LOGICAL/MATHEMATICAL** learning, **BODY/KINESTHETIC** learning, and **VERBAL/LINGUISTIC** learning as children hear the story of Noah and the Great Flood, make drawings depicting several aspects of the story, lay the pictures out in sequence, and walk through the story by explaining the contents of the pictures.

VISUAL/SPATIAL learning: Invite the children individually, in pairs, or in small groups to put the pictures in sequence and tell a brief story about the pictures.

Ask the children to tell you how they knew the sequence of the story from the pictures. Explain that you will now tell them a story of a time when God was angry with the world. Begin by asking the students to listen carefully to the story. When the story is finished, they will have an opportunity to do their own creating by making a large picture book of the story of Noah and the Great Flood.

Begin the story as follows: "After God rested from creating the earth and all that was in it, the human beings that were so lovingly created began to behave in ways that were not pleasing to God. God decided to punish all the people on the earth by causing a great flood that would destroy everything on the earth. But God wanted to save some parts of creation, so God searched and searched and finally found a man who was good and faithful. His name was Noah (picture #1). God called out to Noah (picture #2) and told him to build a boat called an ark (picture #3). While all his neighbors laughed, Noah and his family built a huge ark (picture #4). God told Noah to gather pairs of each kind of animal and bird and take them onto the ark (picture #5). Then it began to rain, and it rained for forty days and forty nights (picture #6). Soon Noah, all his family, and the animals on the ark were the only living people and animals remaining on earth. Everything and everyone else drowned in the water (picture #7)."

Adjust the telling of the story to the age level of your students. Older elementary students can read or listen to the story being read from the Bible.

Assign one child, or several children depending on your class size, to draw one of the seven pictures from the Noah story. Allow time to complete each picture.

Have the children arrange the pictures on the floor in the correct order/sequence of the story. Invite the children one at a time to walk through the story and tell it aloud from the pictures. If your class is large, have the children walk through the story in pairs or small groups and tell one another the story from the pictures. Tell the children you will keep the pictures and review the story because in the next lesson they will discover what happens to Noah and everyone on the ark.

 **VARIATIONS** *Musical/Rhythmic:* Sing "God's Friend Noah" to the tune of "Old MacDonald" (see page 105).

Older children can sing "Rise and Shine." Most children know this song, especially if they have ever been to camp. The song can be shortened by beginning with the chorus. Sing several verses and then add the chorus. The entire story of Noah is told in this song.

Interpersonal: Have children discuss in a small group an animal that may not have made it onto the ark. As a group they can design this animal (perhaps each child can draw a specific part such as the head, body, or legs). They can name and label this animal and display it in the classroom.

Intrapersonal: Have children contemplate what items they would take with them if they were chosen by God to be saved from the destruction of the earth. What are their most valuable possessions?

 **LESSON EVALUATION** See form on page 98.

NOAH AND THE COVENANT

 **SCRIPTURE**   Genesis 8–9:17

 **LESSON FOCUS**   God keeps promises.

 **INTELLIGENCE FOCUS**

INTRAPERSONAL
Interpersonal

 **MATERIALS**

☐ paper
☐ pencils

 **LEARNING AREA**

☐ table for discussing and writing

 **LEARNING PROCESS**   **INTRAPERSONAL** learning combines with **INTERPERSONAL** learning as students recall covenants (promises) they have made and relate these to the covenant that God made with Noah. As they continue to think about interview questions for Noah and develop their own answers based on information from the biblical text and their own imaginations, they will be preparing for the culminating activities of the Noah study in Lesson 4.

 **WARM-UP** | **INTRAPERSONAL** and **INTERPERSONAL** learning: Ask the children what it means to "promise" something. Ask them to reflect on a time when they have made a promise or when someone has made a promise to them. Invite them to share their promise story with a partner or small group.

 **LESSON** | Gather students together and tell them the story (in age-appropriate language) of the raven and the dove that Noah sent out to look for dry land (Gen. 8:6-12). God made a promise, called a covenant, with Noah after the floodwaters had subsided. Read (or tell in age-appropriate words) the covenant story from Genesis 9:8-17. Ask the children to compare what they know about promises they have made and God's promise to Noah.

Ask the children to think about and write questions they might ask Noah about his adventure from the time that God told him to build an ark, until the time that he, his family, and all the animals lived on solid ground again. Then in pairs or small groups discuss the questions, and come up with answers that Noah might have given. Invite the use of imagination as well as the information the children may remember from the story or biblical text.

Tell the students that in the next class everything they have learned about Noah and God's promise will be combined into a written and/or spoken presentation. Invite parents to attend the last ten minutes of the next class for the presentation.

 **VARIATIONS** | *Verbal/Linguistic:* Have older students make journal entries about Noah's days on the ark.

Logical/Mathematical: Have older students calculate the number of days from the start of the rain to the landing of the ark and everyone arriving on dry land.

Visual/Spatial: Have students create additional pictures for the ending of their big book of the Noah story.

Musical/Rhythmic: Have children make a tape of as many of the animal sounds as they can think of that might have been on the ark. If someone has an ocean tape to play in the background (you will need two tape players), record animal sounds over the ocean sound. Use this tape for the presentation for next week.

or

Teach the class "God's Friend Noah."

Verbal/Linguistic and *Body/Kinesthetic:* Have children create a drama about the animals getting restless from being on the ark too long. Act out the story.

 **LESSON EVALUATION** See form on page 98.

LESSON 4

THE NOAH ADVENTURE

 **SCRIPTURE** Genesis 6:1–9:17

 **LESSON FOCUS** Pull together all the information children have learned about Noah.

 **INTELLIGENCE FOCUS**

INTERPERSONAL
Intrapersonal
Verbal/Linguistic
Logical/Mathematical
Musical/Rhythmic
Body/Kinesthetic
Visual/Spatial

MATERIALS

- [ ] paper/pencils
- [ ] audio- or videocassettes
- [ ] simple props or costumes

LEARNING AREA

- [ ] large area with room to walk through the story
- [ ] tables/learning centers to work on activities

  **LEARNING PROCESS** Students will have the opportunity to select the intelligence they wish to work on to prepare a culminating presentation on what they have learned about the story of Noah.

 **WARM-UP** Review the story by walking through the big story-book and verbally telling the story.

 **LESSON** Have the children select one of the following activities to illustrate what they have learned from the previous lessons on Noah.

1. Select one person to be Noah and another to be a reporter from the evening news. Do an interview based on the questions asked in Lesson 3. Record the interview on an audio- or videocassette. (If you are using a video, simple costumes and props add to the excitement.)

2. Write several articles for a newspaper that cover the story of Noah, (e.g., headlines, editorials, personal columns, sports, advertising). Put the articles in a newspaper format and distribute copies to parents and/or the congregation.

3. Write a song, using a familiar tune or a rap, which tells the story of Noah. Include the song/rap in the audio/video presentation. Include the ocean tape with animal sounds on the presentation, or sing "God's Friend Noah."

4. Write a cinquain poem (see sample on page 99) about Noah's adventure with God. Include the poem in the newspaper or in the audio or video presentation.

5. Determine the number of days that passed from the time that God first spoke to Noah until the ark landed on solid ground. Report this information in the newspaper or in the audio/video presentation.

6. Include any journal entries in the newspaper or in the audio/video presentation.

Present the storybook walk-through, the newspaper, and the audio or video account of Noah's adventure with God to parents and or the congregation.

 **LESSON EVALUATION** See form on page 98.

LESSON 5

THE BIRTH OF ISAAC

 **SCRIPTURE**   Genesis 18:1-15; 21:1-3

 **LESSON FOCUS**   God keeps God's promise.

 **INTELLIGENCE FOCUS**   INTERPERSONAL
Body/Kinesthetic
Verbal/Linguistic

 **MATERIALS**    **LEARNING AREA**

- [ ] baby naming book
- [ ] pencils
- [ ] paper
- [ ] simple costumes
- [ ] sheet for a tent
- [ ] baby doll

- [ ] large space for acting out the story
- [ ] tables for writing

 **LEARNING PROCESS**   INTERPERSONAL learning connects with **BODY/KINESTHETIC** learning and **VERBAL/LINGUISTIC** learning as children make connections about what their names mean, and how God chooses names for special people that God has called into service. God kept the promise that was made to Abraham.

 **WARM-UP**

INTERPERSONAL learning: Ask each child to tell the class something about his or her name. Tell each child what the name means from a book of names. Tell them what Jesus' name means.

 **LESSON**

Tell the children that long before Jesus was born, there was a child born whose name was Isaac, which means laughter. Ask the children to listen to the story and try to figure out why Abraham and Sarah named their son Isaac (laughter). Give some background information: Abraham was ninety-nine years old and Sarah was ninety years old. God had promised Abraham that he would be the father of many nations. But Abraham and Sarah waited for years and years without a sign of a child. Now read or tell the story of the visit of the three strangers and of Sarah's reaction to the news that she would be pregnant. Make sure to include the fact that God's promise was kept to Abraham.

For younger children ask them to act out the story with three children being the angels, one old man being Abraham and one old woman being Sarah.

Older children can work together to write a newspaper article about the story: "Ninety-year-old Woman Gives Birth to Son." Some of the children could write a medical report from the hospital. Present the report findings to the class.

 **VARIATIONS**

Musical/Rhythmic learning can be enhanced by a choral reading using voice inflection and sound effects, or a litany of the scripture with a possible response being, "God keeps promises."

Intrapersonal learning can be encouraged as older children write a journal entry from the perspective of Abraham or Sarah about the birth of Isaac.

Logical/Mathematical learning for older children will be increased by comparing what they know about Isaac's birth and Jesus' birth in a Venn diagram (page 100).

Visual/Spatial learning will be enhanced by the children acting out the story in costume.

 **LESSON EVALUATION**

See form on page 98.

LESSON 6

JOSEPH AND HIS BROTHERS

 **SCRIPTURE** Genesis 37:1-36

 **LESSON FOCUS** Joseph is favored by his father and envied by his brothers. God used Joseph.

 **INTELLIGENCE FOCUS**

INTERPERSONAL
Visual/Spatial
Logical/Mathematical
Musical/Rhythmic

MATERIALS

- [ ] large sheets of newsprint
- [ ] markers
- [ ] tagboard cut in three-inch strips
- [ ] crepe paper streamers in various colors
- [ ] glue
- [ ] hole punch
- [ ] string

LEARNING AREA

- [ ] room for students to talk in small groups
- [ ] tables for cutting, pasting, writing

 **LEARNING PROCESS** INTERPERSONAL learning connects with **VISUAL/SPATIAL** and **LOGICAL/MATHEMATICAL** learning as students fit themselves into the story through their own experiences, then draw episodes of the story for others to guess. **VISUAL/SPATIAL** learning is enhanced as students create a multicolored wind sock representing Joseph's coat. **INTRAPERSONAL** learning connects as students become one of the characters in the story and reflect and share feelings about their part in the story. **MUSICAL/RHYTHMIC** learning connects with **INTERPERSONAL** learning as students form groups to write a song or rap about the story.

 **WARM-UP** INTERPERSONAL learning: Ask students to sit in groups of two or three and recall a time when they believed their parent favored a brother or sister over them. Ask them to recall how they felt and what they wanted to do about it.

 **LESSON** Gather the class together and ask them to briefly share their feelings about having someone else favored. Tell them there is an interesting story in the Bible about a boy whose father favored him, and how all his brothers reacted.

Tell the story of Joseph, his dreams, his many-colored coat, his taunting of his brothers and what they did to him from Genesis 37. Tell the story with voice inflection and expression.

Invite students to play Pictionary. Form teams and have them take turns drawing scenes from the story. After one team draws a scene, the other team tries to guess what episode of the story has been drawn.

Invite students to form small groups and write a rap or a song that tells the story of Joseph and his brothers.

Using several colors of crepe paper make a wind sock to represent Joseph's many-colored coat. (See page 108 for sample.) Take a strip of tagboard, and staple the ends to make a circle. Each student will need one wind sock. Allow the children to select as many colored strips of crepe paper as they can fit around the tagboard. Glue the crepe paper strips to the inside of the tagboard ring. Punch three holes in the ring equally distant from one another. Tie strings to each hole and connect them to form a hanger for the wind sock. Display wind socks in your room or the hallways of your church, or have students take them home and tell the story of Joseph and his brothers.

Invite students to select a character in the story (e.g., Joseph, Jacob, or Reuben, and reflect on how that person felt. Invite them to "become" their characters and

33

tell their story to the group. (If your class is large, form two or three small groups so that all the students have an opportunity to participate. Have someone be the recorder and write down basic reflection information. Share the recorded feelings and insights with the total class.)

Verbal/Linguistic: Have students write an account of a part of this story from a particular point of view (examples: Jacob the father, the oldest brother, their mother, and so on).

Body/Kinesthetic: Have students role-play parts of this story.

 See form on page 98.

LESSON 7

RULES TO LIVE BY

 **SCRIPTURE**   Deuteronomy 5:1-21

 **LESSON FOCUS**   God gave us rules to live by.

 **INTELLIGENCE FOCUS**   LOGICAL/
MATHEMATICAL
Visual/Spatial
Verbal/Linguistic

 **MATERIALS**

- [ ] box
- [ ] small ball
- [ ] popsicle sticks
- [ ] copies of a handout listing
  the Ten Commandments
- [ ] paper
- [ ] pencils

 **LEARNING AREA**

- [ ] tables set around the room
  (several may be needed for
  large classes)

 **LEARNING PROCESS**   As children try to play a game with "no rules," **LOGICAL/MATHEMATICAL** learning connects with **VERBAL/LIN-GUISTIC** learning as they share their experiences. This connects with **VISUAL/SPATIAL** learning through guided imagery and provides the setting for **VERBAL/LINGUISTIC** learning in which students create their own set of commandments or rules for today. Which of the Ten Commandments would they

keep? Which would they discard? How would they write rules for themselves and for their world today?

WARM-UP **LOGICAL/MATHEMATICAL** learning: Have children sit around a table. Place the box in the center of the table. Instruct the children that they can play a game for the next five minutes. The game is in the box. Set a timer for five minutes and say, "Go."

LESSON Gather the children together and discuss the game they played. How did it feel to be told to play a game with no rules? What happened? Did you make up your own rules or not play because there were no rules or no goal?

Tell the children they are going to take an imaginary journey through a different kind of day. Invite the children to sit with their hands folded in their laps and their eyes closed. Instruct them to take three deep breaths. Read the following:

"You wake up one morning and begin to dress for school. You go into the kitchen for breakfast and there is nothing on the table and no one around to help you. . . . You open the refrigerator and find only cold macaroni and cheese and diet ginger ale. . . . You decide you aren't hungry and go to catch the school bus across the street. Cars are whizzing by at 75 miles an hour . . . you wonder how you will get across. . . . Finally you cross the street and get on your bus just before it pulls away. . . . The kids are all standing and shouting on the bus. . . . The driver almost hits a car because no one is stopping for lights. . . . Through lots of squealing tires you finally make it to school and you find students rollerblading down the halls, throwing their books and lunches around. . . . You can't wait to get into your classroom . . . when you do, your classmates are sitting on top of desks, ripping up one another's homework and beating up on one another. . . . One boy has a black eye and his mouth is bleeding. . . . Finally it's lunchtime and the kids are all grabbing at food and you almost get hit with someone's baloney sandwich as it flies across the room. . . . All of a sudden you hear your mother's voice . . . she's telling you to wake up or you won't have time for your breakfast before school. . . . You realize that you were having a bad dream. How do you feel? When you are ready, open your eyes and return to our room."

36

Ask the students where they saw/heard the absence of rules. Record responses on a See/Feel T-Chart (see sample on page 103). Ask: "What would the world be like without rules?"

Give the handout of the Ten Commandments to those children who can read. For younger children, use words they can understand to tell them about God's rules for us. Explain that God gave us rules that God wants us to live by. These rules are called the Ten Commandments.

Invite older children to rewrite these commandments in their own language and for their daily world. Invite younger children to tell you in their own words what these commandments mean to them.

Encourage children to talk with their parents about rules to live by.

 *Body/Kinesthetic* and *Musical/Rhythmic:* Write each of the commandments in their numerical order and age-appropriate language on sheets of paper. Place these around the room to create a specific pattern. Have children walk around the room following this pattern. Once the pattern is established, ask them to note each of the commandments and say the commandment in a rhythm as they walk from one to the other. If time allows begin to remove one sheet at a time and see if the children can still remember them from the rhythm and pattern of their walk.

Intrapersonal and *Interpersonal:* Have the children think of each of the commandments using age-appropriate language. Ask them to decide which commandment they keep best, and which one they feel they sometimes break. Give them a few minutes to think about this individually, then ask them to find one or two other people and share their answers.

 See sample on page 98.

RUTH AND NAOMI

 **SCRIPTURE** Ruth 1:1-18

 **LESSON FOCUS** Ruth makes a decision and shows Naomi a special kind of love.

 **INTELLIGENCE FOCUS**

LOGICAL/ MATHEMATICAL
Interpersonal
Verbal/Linguistic
Visual/Spatial
Body/Kinesthetic

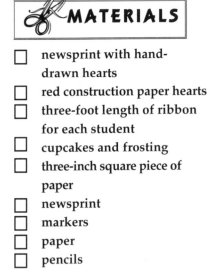 **MATERIALS**

- [ ] newsprint with hand-drawn hearts
- [ ] red construction paper hearts
- [ ] three-foot length of ribbon for each student
- [ ] cupcakes and frosting
- [ ] three-inch square piece of paper
- [ ] newsprint
- [ ] markers
- [ ] paper
- [ ] pencils

LEARNING AREA

- [ ] space for students to sit in pairs
- [ ] space for students to work in small groups

 **LEARNING PROCESS** LOGICAL/MATHEMATICAL learning connects with **INTERPERSONAL** learning as students think and discuss decisions they would make. **VERBAL/LINGUISTIC** learning connects with **VISUAL/SPATIAL** learning as students talk about different kinds of love and create a ribbon of hearts. **BODY/KINESTHETIC** learning connects with **VERBAL/LINGUISTIC** learning as students write love messages and frost cupcakes as love gifts. **VERBAL/LINGUISTIC** learning connects with **VISUAL/SPATIAL** and **LOGICAL/MATHEMATICAL** learning as students create and do a wall-size word search.

 **WARM-UP** Ask students to sit in pairs and decide on one of the following options. Ask the following questions: Would you rather:

- go to the beach with your parents or the park with a friend?
- take care of a friend's pet or go to a movie?
- make a card for your aunt in the hospital or do homework?
- play ball with your friends or bake cookies with your mother?

Allow a brief time for each decision to be made and discussed. Tell your students they will hear a story about a young woman who made a decision based on love that changed her life.

 **LESSON** Tell the story of Ruth and Naomi to your students. If you are comfortable doing so, tell the story in the first person as Ruth or Naomi dressed in costume (a costume can be a simple head shawl). At the end of the story tell the students that this was a very special kind of love between two people.

Ask the students for examples of all the kinds of love they can think of (husband/wife, brother/sister, parent/child, pets, God/us, and so on). Record each kind of love on a heart on newsprint or a chalkboard. Tell students God created many kinds of love and we need to be as loving as we can to all God's creatures.

Invite students to create a heart streamer by writing the names of people or pets they love on hearts (precut for young students) and stapling the hearts to a ribbon. Hang the heart-filled ribbon from the ceiling so that the room is filled with love.

Invite students to write a love message to someone special on three-inch pieces of paper. Frost the cupcakes (or actually bake the cupcakes during the lesson). Roll up the love message and gently push it into the top of the cupcake. Students can hand deliver this special gift of love. Allow for more than one cupcake per child so they can give away several.

Older students can work together to create a wall-size word search by using a prelined sheet of newsprint and adding words such as: COMMITMENT, COURAGE, LOVE, DECISION, RISK, RUTH, JOURNEY, NAOMI, ORPAH, and any other words they think go along with the story. Once these words have been placed on the word search page, they can fill in the remaining spaces with letters. Be sure to make a list of the words to search for.

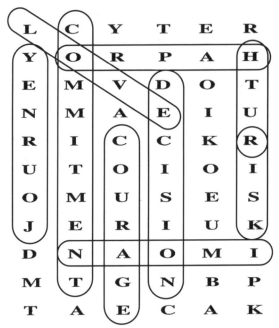

L	C	Y	T	E	R
Y	O	R	P	A	H
E	M	V	D	O	T
N	M	A	E	I	U
R	I	C	C	K	R
U	T	O	I	O	I
O	M	U	S	E	S
J	E	R	I	U	K
D	N	A	O	M	I
M	T	G	N	B	P
T	A	E	C	A	K

VARIATIONS

Musical/Rhythmic: Have students develop new words for the song "He's Got the Whole World in His Hands" to fit the theme of this story.

Verbal/Linguistic: Have students write a cinquain poem about love (see sample on page 99).

Intrapersonal: Have students write a letter to a friend as either Ruth or Naomi telling about their decision-making day.

LESSON EVALUATION

See form on page 98.

LESSON 9

THE LORD IS MY SHEPHERD

 **SCRIPTURE** Psalm 23

 **LESSON FOCUS** God takes care of us always.

 **INTELLIGENCE FOCUS** INTRAPERSONAL
Verbal/Linguistic
Visual/Spatial
Body/Kinesthetic

 **MATERIALS**

- [ ] paper/pencils
- [ ] sheep (or pet animal)
- [ ] fingerpaint (or pistachio pudding)
- [ ] fingerpaint paper or shelf paper (or paper plate if you are using pudding)

 **LEARNING AREA**

- [ ] tables located around the room
- [ ] large space for animal and keeper

 **LEARNING PROCESS** INTRAPERSONAL learning connects with **VERBAL/LINGUISTIC** learning, **VISUAL/SPATIAL** learning, and **BODY/KINESTHETIC** learning as children discover what it means to have someone take care of them and to care for someone or something. A connection is made to the way God takes care of each of us as described in Psalm 23.

 **INTRAPERSONAL** learning: When students arrive, ask them to answer the following questions. Who takes care of you? Who do you take care of? What does it mean to take care of someone or something? Where do you feel safe? Students may share their answers in a discussion.

 Choose the following option that is most logical for you and your students, depending on your geographic area.

Invite (several weeks in advance) a shepherd, someone from a petting zoo, a veterinarian, or someone who owns a pet to come and share with your class about caring for an animal. If possible, have the sheep or other animal present. This will add another dimension of learning as children see and touch the animal.

Relate the information about caring for a sheep or other animal to the questions asked earlier about who takes care of you. Are there similarities? Differences?

Read or ask a student to read Psalm 23. Ask children how God in this psalm is like someone who cares for them.

Invite children to either use fingerpaints or pistachio pudding to "paint their feelings" after hearing this psalm or write a cinquain poem (see page 99) about a God who cares so much for us.

Display the children's artwork or poems around the room. Invite parents to view these productions, and encourage them to ask the children to relate what they have learned.

 *Logical/Mathematical:* Have children think of and create a list of all the things involved with caring for a sheep (or pet). Then ask them to create a list of all the things God does to care for us. Younger children can compare their lists to find the ways that caring for pets is the same as God's care for us. Older children can create a Venn diagram (see page 100) to show similarities and differences.

Musical/Rhythmic and *Intrapersonal:* Play a tape of pastoral music (a gentle piece of music suggesting the calmness of the countryside; from the Latin *pastor,* meaning shepherd). Invite the children to read the psalm to themselves as they listen to the music to create an atmosphere of peace and calmness. When they finish reading the psalm, invite them to remain still and listen to the music as they reflect on the words they have just read.

For younger children, read the psalm to them. Have them think about the psalm as they listen to the music. Ask the children to remain quiet and think about the words of the psalm.

 **LESSON EVALUATION** See form on page 98.

LESSON 10

THE PROPHET JONAH

 **SCRIPTURE**   Jonah 1:1–4:11

 **LESSON FOCUS**   We need to obey God.

 **INTELLIGENCE FOCUS**

INTERPERSONAL
Body/Kinesthetic
Verbal/Linguistic
Visual/Spatial

 **MATERIALS**

- [ ] cue card with UH-OH printed on one side and YEAH! printed on the other (color-coded for younger children)
- [ ] materials for props for use as land, a boat, and a fish
- [ ] paper and markers for drawing the story (for younger children)

 **LEARNING AREA**

- [ ] large area to re-enact the story of Jonah
- [ ] table for writing and drawing

 **LEARNING PROCESS**

INTERPERSONAL learning connects with BODY/KINESTHETIC, VERBAL/LIN-GUISTIC and VISUAL/ SPATIAL learning as children get involved with the story of Jonah and then re-create it as three scenes and tell their part of the story.

WARM-UP INTERPERSONAL learning: Invite children to share with a partner a story about a time when they disobeyed a command from someone—a parent, teacher, or other adult. Ask them to explain what the command was, and what they did instead. What were the consequences?

LESSON Gather the students together in a large group and tell the story of Jonah using a cue card that says UH-OH on the front and YEAH! on the back. Practice having the children say in very dramatic voices UH-OH and YEAH! as you flip the card. Tell them that as you read the story, you will stop and hold up the card. They are to say what is on the card.

The Story of Jonah

One day God saw Jonah walking along the road and said to him, "Go to Nineveh, the great city, and speak out against it; I am aware of how bad its people are." UH-OH. Jonah didn't want to go to Nineveh, so he disobeyed God, went the opposite direction, and got on a boat sailing for Spain. UH-OH. God sent a mighty storm that tossed the ship around and everyone was frightened. UH-OH. Jonah had fallen asleep and the captain of the ship found him . . . UH-OH . . . and told him to pray to his God to save them. The sailors discovered that Jonah was to blame for the storm because he tried to run away from God. UH-OH. The sailors told him that was a bad thing to do. Jonah told them to throw him overboard . . . UH-OH, and they did. UH-OH. But God had mercy on Jonah . . . YEAH! and sent a huge fish (like a whale) to swallow Jonah. UH-OH.

Jonah lived in the belly of the fish for three days and three nights. UH-OH. Jonah prayed to God while he was in the belly of the fish. YEAH! God made the fish spit Jonah up onto dry land. YEAH! Once again God spoke to Jonah saying, "Go to Nineveh, that great city and tell the people the message I have given you." UH-OH. This time Jonah obeyed God's word. YEAH! He told the people of Nineveh that God would destroy their city if they did not obey. UH-OH. They did obey God and stopped their wicked ways. YEAH! God taught Jonah a lesson about obeying God and loving his enemies. YEAH!

Divide older children into three groups and let them depict a part of the story.

- *Group 1* will have dry land—where God spoke to Jonah (1:1-3*a*, and 2:10–3:3). The rest of the story (3:4–4:11) may be acted out if time allows.
- *Group 2* will have the ship (1:3*b*-16).

- *Group 3* will have the belly of the great fish (1:17–2:9).

Invite each group to work together to design their props, and to decide on how they will tell their portion of the story. Allow the groups enough time to prepare their set area and to decide on a storytelling method. Allow each group to present their part of the story.

Younger children can also work in three groups and prepare a mural by creating three separate pictures to tell the story of Jonah. Allow time for the children to create the three story portions and tell their part of the story of Jonah.

Invite parents or another class to see and hear the presentation of the story.

 *Logical/Mathematical:* Have students find Israel on a map. Trace Jonah's journey to Joppa, into the Mediterranean Sea, back to the land, and to Nineveh in the Assyrian Empire.

Musical/Rhythmic: Have students create a song or a rap to tell the story of Jonah. If you are presenting this story to another class or group, use this musical piece as a part of the presentation.

Intrapersonal: Ask students to write or journal about a time when they disobeyed, or about what Jonah might have thought about while he was in the belly of the fish.

 See form on page 98.

LESSON 11

JESUS IS BORN

 **SCRIPTURE** Luke 2:1-20

 **LESSON FOCUS** God's Son, our Lord and Savior, is born.

 **INTELLIGENCE FOCUS** MUSICAL/RHYTHMIC
Interpersonal
Verbal/Linguistic
Visual/Spatial

 **MATERIALS**

- ☐ paper for writing and drawing
- ☐ pencils
- ☐ hymnals
- ☐ newsprint
- ☐ markers
- ☐ tape of Christmas music
- ☐ tape player

 **LEARNING AREA**

- ☐ floor space for sitting
- ☐ tables to write on

 **LEARNING PROCESS** MUSICAL/RHYTHMIC learning connects with **INTERPERSONAL, VERBAL/LIN-GUISTIC** and **VISUAL/ SPATIAL** learning as children become engaged in the story of the birth of Jesus through music, teamwork, and writing or illustrating a story or song.

 **WARM-UP** VERBAL/LINGUISTIC learning: Divide your class into teams of five (older elementary) or three (younger elementary) students. Ask "I'm thinking of . . ." questions about popular songs. Think of a number between one and twelve. The team that chooses the number closest to your number gets to ask the first question. Set a time limit for writing questions and play the game.

After the game ask the children to think of songs or hymns that they have heard or sung about Jesus' birth. List the titles on newsprint. Older children can use a hymnal to find song titles.

 **LESSON** Read or tell the story of Jesus' birth from the second chapter of Luke. Ask the children to review their song or hymn list, and to listen for ways that the titles may fit into the story.

Move the children back into their teams. Ask them to write the story of the birth of Jesus, and to use as many song titles as possible to tell the story. Or use a familiar hymn to write a song that includes titles of songs about the birth of Jesus.

Younger children can illustrate a Christmas hymn. Ask an adult to write a phrase from the chorus of a familiar hymn and let the children create a picture to illustrate the words.

These stories or songs can be posted around the room or on a hallway bulletin board, used to make greeting cards, or used as the bulletin cover for your Christmas Eve service.

 **VARIATIONS** *Logical/Mathematical:* Have children create a word search for their classmates or parents that has at least fifteen Christmas words in it. Or create an acrostic of the word *Christmas.*

Intrapersonal: Ask the children to create a Christmas card for someone special with a personal note about what Christmas means to them.

Body/Kinesthetic: Have children dance to Christmas songs. Invite them to move to the music however they feel it, or create a special dance to go with the rhythm.

 **LESSON EVALUATION** See form on page 98.

THE VISIT OF THE MAGI

 **SCRIPTURE** | Matthew 2:1-12

 **LESSON FOCUS**

The visit of the wise men proclaims to the world that Jesus' birth is a very special occurrence.

 **INTELLIGENCE FOCUS**

BODY/KINESTHETIC
Intrapersonal
Visual/Spatial

MATERIALS

- [ ] stars of graduating sizes
- [ ] manger scene (pictures or a crèche)
- [ ] light blue, black, and white construction paper
- [ ] pencils
- [ ] newsprint
- [ ] wise men (silhouette patterns)
- [ ] camel
- [ ] star patterns
- [ ] glue

LEARNING AREA

- [ ] stars placed around the room (small stars graduated to larger stars) ending over a picture or actual crèche scene
- [ ] space where children can move around
- [ ] tables and chairs for writing and constructing

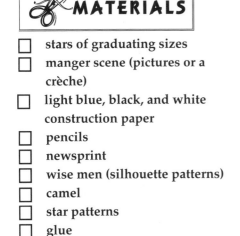  **LEARNING PROCESS**

BODY/KINESTHETIC learning connects with INTRAPERSONAL learning and VISUAL/SPATIAL learning as children move their bodies through the story of the visit of the Magi, think about what they may have seen/felt/heard, and make a silhouette design of the three wise men.

WARM-UP

BODY/KINESTHETIC learning: Ask the children to pretend they are going on a long vacation. Ask: What will you need? How do you feel about taking this trip? Then ask them to show with their bodies how they might look if they were taking this trip riding on: an elephant, a racing horse, a stalking tiger, a jumping rabbit, or a rocking camel.

Talk about how it would feel to ride those different animals on a very long journey.

LESSON

Invite children to follow the stars around the room as the stars get bigger. Ask where they think this trip is taking them. Sit in front of the picture or real crèche and tell the children that when Jesus was born some men followed a star as they rode on camels for a very long distance. They used the star to guide them to where Jesus was. Read or tell the story of the visit of the wise men from Matthew's Gospel (2:1-12). Read or tell the story again, asking the children to pretend with their whole bodies that they are riding camels. As they quietly ride, ask them to listen for things they can see and hear.

Have younger children make a T-Chart on newsprint (see page 103) to record what they saw or heard during the story. Ask them to use their imaginations and list as many things as they can.

Have older children make a chart with five columns. Title the columns with the five senses (saw, heard, smelled, touched, and tasted). Ask them to record in columns what they saw/heard/smelled/touched/tasted during the story.

Using the paper, patterns, glue, and pencils invite children to create a picture with silhouettes of the wise men, camels, star. Younger children will need help cutting.

The creations of the children can be made into an Epiphany bulletin board, decorations for your classroom, or as an invitation to an Epiphany party.

 **VARIATIONS** *Verbal/Linguistic, Musical/Rhythmic,* and *Interpersonal:* Invite children to work in small groups as they tell the story of the visit of the Magi. Record the story-telling and provide sound effects while they talk.

Musical/Rhythmic and *Visual/Spatial:* Create an illustrated hymn using pictures or a rebus story to depict the words of "We Three Kings."

Logical/Mathematical: Use a map or globe and have students trace the journey of the Magi from the Far East (China) to Bethlehem (Israel).

 **LESSON EVALUATION** See form on page 98.

LESSON 13

JESUS' BAPTISM

 **SCRIPTURE** Mark 1:9-11

 **LESSON FOCUS** Jesus' ministry begins with the proclamation that he is God's Son.

INTELLIGENCE FOCUS
BODY/KINESTHETIC
Visual/Spatial
Intrapersonal
Verbal/Linguistic
Logical/Mathematical

 **MATERIALS**

- [ ] bowl
- [ ] water
- [ ] towel
- [ ] items that float or sink (animal sponges, plastic tape, coins, marbles, etc.)
- [ ] Venn diagram worksheet (see page 100)
- [ ] pencils
- [ ] masking tape
- [ ] blue construction paper for constructing a Jordan River

LEARNING AREA

- [ ] space for children to walk on the construction paper Jordan River and touch the water
- [ ] tables and chairs
- [ ] space for working on a large Venn diagram constructed from masking tape

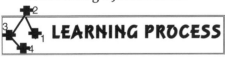 **LEARNING PROCESS**

BODY/KINESTHETIC learning connects with **VISUAL/SPATIAL** and **INTRA-PERSONAL** learning as children use pictures/articles from their baptism to remember it, and as they walk along a construction paper Jordan River to the bowl to dip their hands into water as a kinesthetic reminder of baptism. **VERBAL/LINGUISTIC** learning connects with **LOGICAL/MATHEMATICAL** learning as they talk about their own baptism and connect it with differences and similarities to Jesus' baptism through Venn diagrams.

 **BODY/KINESTHETIC** learning: Place a large basin of water on a table. Invite the children to "play" with the water by discovering which items float or sink. Set a time limit of 2 to 3 minutes.

 Gather the children together and ask them to think of the various uses of water. Encourage lots of right answers. List their answers on newsprint. Older children can be encouraged to categorize their answers in groups (e.g., fun activities, cleansing activities).

Tell them that water was very important when Jesus lived because his country was mostly a desert. Tell or read them the story of Jesus' baptism in the Jordan River from Mark's Gospel.

Using age-appropriate language, explain what the word *baptism* means and the reason people are baptized. Ask the children to share something they know about their own baptism How old were they? Where was it done? Who baptized them? Who was there to celebrate their baptism?

Read or tell (for younger children) about your church's baptismal service. Now invite children one by one to walk along the construction paper Jordan River and to dip their hand into a bowl of fresh water and touch their head or their heart. Ask them to think about what their baptism means and the significance of the promise their parents made for them. Allow quiet time to think and reflect. If there are children who have not been baptized ask them to think of a time when they witnessed a baptism and what it might mean to the families who were involved.

Use masking tape to make 2 large circles (approximately 10 feet in diameter) on the floor. The Venn diagram on page 100 shows where the circles connect. Ask younger children to stand on a large floor model two-sphere Venn diagram labeled Jesus' baptism and their baptism. Ask them to stand in the circle that represents Jesus' baptism as you have them recall the story. Next, have them stand in the circle marked their baptism as they talk about what they know about it. Ask them to stand in the connecting piece of the circles as they listen for things that were true of both Jesus' baptism and their own (e.g., both used water, both had someone else do the baptizing, both had other people around).

Ask older children to write words or draw pictures on a two-sphere Venn diagram of Jesus' baptism and their own baptism, making sure to fill in the center area of commonalities.

Invite children to talk with their parents (and sponsors if they had them) about their baptism.

 **VARIATIONS** *Interpersonal:* Invite a family with a young child who has been baptized recently. Ask them to bring the baby and talk to the class about why they had their child baptized.

Musical/Rhythmic: Sing or read to rhythm a favorite baptismal hymn (example: "Child of Blessing, Child of Promise"). Create a bulletin board or posterboard of pictures with a copy of the hymn in the center. Older children can discuss what the hymn means as they work.

 **LESSON EVALUATION** See form on page 98.

COME, FOLLOW ME

 **SCRIPTURE** Matthew 4:18-22; 9:9

 **LESSON FOCUS** Many different people chose to follow Jesus.

 **INTELLIGENCE FOCUS** VISUAL/SPATIAL
Logical/Mathematical
Interpersonal
Verbal/Linguistic
Body/Kinesthetic
Intrapersonal

 **MATERIALS**

- [ ] paper
- [ ] markers
- [ ] yarn in different colors
- [ ] stamp pad
- [ ] magnifying glass

LEARNING AREA

- [ ] space for playing follow the leader
- [ ] tables for writing and drawing
- [ ] bulletin board or display area

 **LEARNING PROCESS**

VISUAL/SPATIAL learning connects with **LOGICAL/MATHEMATICAL** and **INTERPERSONAL** learning as students discover and compare their own similarities and differences in groups. **VERBAL/LINGUISTIC** learning connects with **VISUAL/SPATIAL** learning as students write or talk about their own uniqueness and ways they can follow Jesus. **BODY/**

55

KINESTHETIC connects with **INTRAPERSONAL** learning as students discover and reflect on what it means to both lead and follow.

 **VISUAL/SPATIAL** learning: Play a game of follow the leader. Allow several different students to be the leader. If you have a large class, form two or three groups to allow more students to participate as leaders. Play the game in one-minute intervals per leader. At the end of five minutes, sit down and discuss how it felt to be a leader, and how it felt to be a follower. Tell the students that Jesus was one of the world's great leaders. The people who followed him were dedicated and very different from one another.

 Tell the story from Matthew's Gospel of Jesus calling Peter, Andrew, James, John, and Matthew. The first four men were fishermen, the last man was a tax collector. Tell your students that fishing was hard, rough work, and tax collecting was a profession that was hated by all the people. Ask older students to name the other disciples.

Ask students to work in groups of three or four to discuss what it means to follow Jesus. Create a group list of answers. Use words for older students and pictures for younger students.

Have students make an imprint of their thumb with a stamp pad on the top half of a sheet of paper. Using a magnifying glass, check out one another's thumbprints to find differences and similarities. Invite students to make characters of themselves out of their thumbprints and write the words, "I am a follower of Jesus" on the bottom, top, or side of the paper. Divide the bottom half of the paper into two. In the left column ask students to list some of their unique characteristics such as: good at baseball, likes to sing, plays a tuba. In the other column invite students to list ways that they can follow Jesus.

Younger children can make thumbprints with their names and place them on a bulletin board that says "I am a follower of Jesus." Encourage them to add special qualities like: hair color, freckles, dimples. Look at the differences and similarities between the groups. Ask each student to tell you how they can follow Jesus. Write their statements next to their picture.

 *Verbal/Linguistic:* Have students research other persons who were followers of Jesus to find out similarities and differences. Share the information with the group.

Musical/Rhythmic: Have students create a chant or rhythm to the words "come, follow me." Discover how many rhythms can be created using those three words.

 **LESSON EVALUATION** See form on page 98.

LESSON 15

JESUS AND THE CHILDREN

 **SCRIPTURE** Mark 10:13-16

 **LESSON FOCUS** Children were important to Jesus and are important in the church today.

 **INTELLIGENCE FOCUS**

INTRAPERSONAL
Body/Kinesthetic
Visual/Spatial
Interpersonal
Verbal/Linguistic

MATERIALS

- [ ] large paper for mural
- [ ] smaller paper for drawings
- [ ] markers
- [ ] scissors
- [ ] tape/glue
- [ ] tape recorder and cassette tape
- [ ] paper
- [ ] pencils

LEARNING AREA

- [ ] space for students to sit quietly
- [ ] area for role-playing the story
- [ ] wall space for hanging a large picture

 **LEARNING PROCESS**

INTRAPERSONAL learning connects with **BODY/KINESTHETIC** learning as students visualize the story in their minds and then role-play the story. **VISUAL/SPATIAL** learning connects with **INTER-PERSONAL** learning as students work together to create a mural. **INTERPER-SONAL** learning connects with **VERBAL/LINGUISTIC** learning as students interview adults, record their responses, and create a web of children in church.

 Have the students sit quietly with their feet on the floor, hands in their laps, and their eyes closed. Say, "Take three deep breaths (allow time). Listen to the sound of my voice and try to see a picture in your mind's eye as I tell you a story. Picture yourself on a picnic. . . . See the grass and trees around you. . . . Feel the fuzziness of the blanket you are sitting on. . . . Hear other children laughing and playing on the swings. . . . Feel yourself swinging high into the sky. . . . Smell the food cooking on the grill. . . . Taste some of the snacks as you wait for your food to cook. . . . Look at everyone who is around you and smile at them. . . . When you are ready, open your eyes and come back to our room."

Invite students to tell you about this experience. Ask what they saw, heard, smelled, and felt.

 Invite students to stand up and stretch. Tell them you are going to ask them to see another story in their minds. Once again have them sit very still, feet on the floor, hands in their laps, eyes closed. Now say, "Take three deep breaths (allow time). See a hillside with many people. See Jesus sitting on the ground talking to the people. . . . What does he look like? What does his voice sound like? See mothers come through the crowd with their children. . . . How many children are there? Many? Just one or two? How old are they? Are they quiet or noisy? Are they boys or girls? Now hear some men yelling at the children to go away. . . . How do the children look now? Are they frightened? Now hear Jesus saying, 'Let the children come to me; do not stop them; because the kingdom belongs to such as these.' Now see Jesus take all the children into his arms, hug them, and bless them. . . . How do the children look now? How do the men, the disciples look now? How does Jesus look now? When you are ready, open your eyes and slowly come back to our room."

Invite students to tell you about this experience. Ask what they saw and heard, and how they felt about the story.

Invite students to select characters and act out the story (Jesus, the disciples, parents, and children). Older students can create their own dialogue, while younger students can act out the parts while the teacher reads or tells the story.

Have each student draw a picture of herself or himself to be placed on a large mural-size poster. Invite one student to draw Jesus and place him in the picture. Invite other students to create the background (grass, trees, other people in the background).

Older students can tape-record interviews with adults, including the pastor, about this question, "How do children make this church a better place?" The class can listen to the responses to the interview and transcribe the information for the church newsletter.

Older students can work together to create a concept map about how children can make church a better place. (See page 102.)

 *Musical/Rhythmic:* Younger students can sing "Jesus Loves Me." Older students can create a new beat or tune for the words to that song.

Logical/Mathematical: Create a list of reasons why children need to be a part of the church today.

 See form on page 98.

LESSON 16

JESUS CALMS THE STORM

 **SCRIPTURE** Mark 4:35-41

 **LESSON FOCUS** Jesus is God's Son and has mighty power even over the wind and sea.

INTELLIGENCE FOCUS

BODY/KINESTHETIC
Logical/Mathematical
Intrapersonal
Musical/Rhythmic
Interpersonal

 **MATERIALS**

- [ ] several library books about fishing boats
- [ ] masking tape
- [ ] rulers
- [ ] yardsticks or measuring tape
- [ ] audiocassette player
- [ ] cassette tape
- [ ] Bible
- [ ] materials for sound effects
- [ ] pillow

LEARNING AREA

- [ ] tables around the walls of the room
- [ ] large open space for outline of the boat

 **LEARNING PROCESS**

LOGICAL/MATHEMATICAL learning connects with **BODY/ KINESTHETIC** learning and **INTRAPERSONAL** learning as children (on their own or with the help of the teacher) discover the dimensions of a typical fishing boat in Jesus' time, simulate the experience of the fishing boat, and reflect on their feelings. **INTERPERSONAL** learning connects with **MUSICAL/ RHYTHMIC** learning as children work together to create sound effects for the storm.

BODY/KINESTHETIC learning: Play a game of Simon Says with the children to get them used to moving their bodies. Then ask them to show you with their body positions someone who is:

very cold	on a swaying boat
very tired	hot and thirsty
frightened	awakened quickly

Talk about what it felt like/looked like to say something with your body.

Have several books available from the church or public library. Help children find and read about the size and shape of a fishing boat similar to one that Jesus might have been in. Explain that they are doing research in order to build a make-believe boat like the one that Jesus and his disciples were in during the storm.

With rulers, yardsticks, or measuring tape, ask students to measure the dimensions of the boat. Use masking tape to mark the outline of the boat on the floor.

Decide who will be Jesus. Instruct this child to act out being rudely awakened, standing up, and telling the wind and sea to be calm.

Invite twelve (or as many as you have) other students to sit in the "boat" marked out on the floor. The one who is Jesus will need a pillow and pretend to sleep.

Other students may work in a small group to create the storm—complete with pounding surf, creaking wood, flapping sails, and moans and groans of fear. Record these sounds on the cassette tape. If you do not have extra students, pre-record sounds of the children being in the storm as an alternative exercise for those who do not wish to do research on the boat. Or find a nature tape of a storm and create other sound effects to go along with it.

When you have set the stage and had the children practice being in a fishing boat, read the beginning of the story from Mark's Gospel (4:35-37), and ask the children to pretend that they are in a boat on a stormy lake. Ask them to sway in the boat as if it was being tossed around in a storm. Darken the room as much as possible. Play the storm sounds. Flick the lights on and off to simulate lightning.

Read the rest of the scripture lesson (4:38-41). Ask students to react as they would in the story by feeling the fear in their bodies. Someone then wakes Jesus, and as he speaks, all movement and sound stop.

Ask students to reflect on their experience in the fishing boat:

- What did it feel like in the storm?
- Were you afraid?
- What were your feelings about Jesus during the storm when he was asleep?
- How did you feel when he commanded the storm to stop and it did?

Invite students to think carefully about each question. This is an inner journey. Allow time for sharing. Remember, there are no right or wrong answers when children share their thoughts and feelings.

Invite children to share this story with their parents, telling them about their experience with the storm.

 **VARIATIONS**

Verbal/Linguistic: Have students create an evening news presentation about the storm, including a weather report, eyewitness reports, and a human interest report.

Visual/Spatial: Have students make pictures of the storm, including Jesus in the boat.

 **LESSON EVALUATION**

See form on page 98.

THE FEEDING OF THE FIVE THOUSAND

 **SCRIPTURE** John 6:1-14

 **LESSON FOCUS** Jesus produced a miracle by feeding over five thousand people with very little food.

 **INTELLIGENCE FOCUS**

INTERPERSONAL
Body/Kinesthetic
Logical/Mathematical
Visual/Spatial
Intrapersonal
Verbal/Linguistic

 **MATERIALS**

- [ ] paper
- [ ] markers
- [ ] snack food (two apples and three graham crackers for a class of ten students)
- [ ] knife
- [ ] napkins
- [ ] What, So What, Now What? Chart (see page 104)

LEARNING AREA

- [ ] space for students to sit in a circle and play "I'm Going on a Picnic"

 **LEARNING PROCESS** BODY/KINESTHETIC learning connects with VERBAL/LINGUISTIC learning as students hear and act out in a echo-pantomime the story of the feeding of the five thousand. VISUAL/SPATIAL learning connects with LOGICAL/MATHEMATICAL learning as students draw pictures of the story and put them in sequence. LOGICAL/MATHEMATICAL learning connects with INTRAPERSONAL and INTERPERSONAL learning as students share a snack, express how they felt about the exercise, and how it relates to their own lives.

 **WARM-UP** INTERPERSONAL and LOGICAL/MATHEMATICAL learning: Have the students sit in a circle and play "I'm Going on a Picnic." Explain the rules of this game. One person begins with the phrase, "I'm going on a picnic, and I'm bringing potato salad." (Use any other appropriate item to bring on a picnic that begins with the letter *P*.) The next person says, "I'm going on a picnic and I'm bringing potato salad and. . . ." (Use anything appropriate that begins with the letter *I*. Continue the game until you have spelled the word *picnic*.) Each student must repeat all of the items already mentioned. (If your class is large divide the students into groups. If you have nonreaders, give them the letter they need to play.) After the game tell the students you are going to tell them the story of the world's largest picnic.

LESSON Tell the story from John's Gospel using an echo-pantomime.

One day a large crowd gathered
(Extend arms out wide.)

To hear Jesus teach.
(Cup hand to ear to indicate listening.)

It was getting late.
(Look at wristwatch.)

And this large crowd was getting hungry.
(Rub stomach area to indicate hunger.)

Jesus said, "Feed them."
(Hands around mouth to indicate talking.)

The disciples said there was not enough food.
(Shrug shoulders and shake head.)

65

A small boy had five loaves and two fishes.
(Hold up five fingers and two fingers.)

Jesus prayed over the food.
(Fold hands and bow head in prayer.)

And distributed it to all of the people.
(Pretend to hand out food.)

They were all full.
(Hand over stomach area and big smile on face.)

And there were twelve baskets left over.
(Pretend to collect leftovers.)

The crowd knew they had seen a miracle.
(Lift hands and face to heaven.)

Have paper and markers or crayons available for students to work in small groups and draw pictures of the events of the story.

Older students might draw sequence frames of the story; younger students might draw one aspect of the story and put the pictures in order when they have finished.

In a large class invite small groups of students to tell the story to their class (or another class) using their pictures to guide the storytelling, or using the echo-pantomime.

Give one or two students a small amount of food to share with the class. Ask the students to discover ways to share this small amount of food with all the students. Then decide as a class how to divide up the food.

Ask students to reflect on how it felt when they saw how little food there was, and how they felt when they came up with ways to share it. After a few minutes of reflection, ask them to share their thoughts with the group. Ask how this story affects their daily lives. How can they share what they have so that others can be helped? Ask each student to create a What, So What, Now What? chart to share with the class.

 *Musical/Rhythmic:* Write a song or rap to tell the story.

Verbal/Linguistic: Create a rebus story with words and pictures.

 See form on page 98.

THE HEALING OF THE PARALYZED MAN

 **SCRIPTURE**   Mark 2:1-12

 **LESSON FOCUS**   Jesus has the power to heal.

 **INTELLIGENCE FOCUS**

VISUAL/SPATIAL
Musical/Rhythmic
Intrapersonal
Interpersonal

 **MATERIALS**

- [ ] picture of a crowd scene
- [ ] enlarged picture of the healing of the paralyzed man
- [ ] shoe box
- [ ] string
- [ ] paper
- [ ] markers
- [ ] several copies of the words to "Jesus Healed Him" (See page 105.)

LEARNING AREA

- [ ] tables
- [ ] chairs

 **LEARNING PROCESS**

VISUAL/SPATIAL learning connects with INTRAPERSONAL and INTER-PERSONAL learning as children decide who they would be in the warm-up picture and the picture of the healing of the paralyzed man. **MUSICAL/RHYTHMIC** learning engages children as they sing the story to a familiar tune.

WARM-UP

VISUAL/SPATIAL learning: Show the children a picture in which there are people both participating and watching (parade, circus, sports event). Ask the children to look at the picture and decide who they would be in the picture. Would they be standing in the crowd watching? Would they be at the center of the action? Would they be people helping? Ask them to think about what role they would be playing and why. Have them share their answers with a partner.

LESSON

Gather the children together and sing the chorus to "Jesus Loves Me." Now, using the same tune, sing "Jesus Healed Him," a song about Jesus healing a man who was paralyzed. Hand out copies of the words to older children, or sing it through several times for younger children.

Read or tell the story of the healing of the paralyzed man from Mark's Gospel.

Show older children Annie Volitin's line drawing of the healing of the paralyzed man from the *Good News Bible*. Ask older elementary children where they are in the picture. Are they the crowd, the friends, the paralyzed man himself? In small groups, invite them to share their answers and tell why.

Ask younger children to make a diorama of this story using a shoe box (or other box). Cut a hole through the roof and use string and other materials to make this scene. Older children may be intrigued by this project and add more detail and materials.

VARIATIONS

Verbal/Linguistic: Using the story grid form on page 101, have the children write a modern-day version of the story. List categories such as "situation, sick person, ways friends helped, crowd reactions."

Logical/Mathematical: Invite children to think of other ways to get the paralyzed man into the house so Jesus could heal him. Invite them to come up with other ways Jesus' healing could take place.

Verbal/Linguistic and *Body/Kinesthetic:* Invite children to write a script using their own words to tell the story. Have children role-play the drama of friends carrying a paralyzed man to Jesus (be careful that children do not get hurt carrying another child). Discuss the experience.

Body/Kinesthetic: Invite children to create a "machine" with their bodies. This machine can have moving parts (that may make noises) to lower the paralyzed man down through the roof.

 **LESSON EVALUATION**   See form on page 98.

LESSON 19

THE GOOD SAMARITAN

 **SCRIPTURE**   Luke 10:25-37

LESSON FOCUS   Who is my neighbor?

 **INTELLIGENCE FOCUS**

LOGICAL/ MATHEMATICAL
Body/Kinesthetic
Verbal/Linguistic
Interpersonal

 **MATERIALS**

- [ ] slip of paper
- [ ] pencils
- [ ] sequencing cards
  (see pages 17-18)
- [ ] story grid
  (see page 101)
- [ ] paper
- [ ] pencils
- [ ] chalkboard or newsprint

 **LEARNING AREA**

- [ ] chairs and tables for writing
- [ ] open space for role play

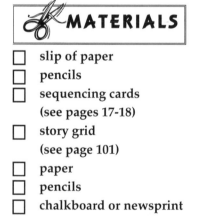  **LEARNING PROCESS**

LOGICAL/MATHEMATICAL learning connects with **BODY/KINESTHETIC** learning as children learn sequencing in the acting out of Luke's parable. They will then connect with **VERBAL/ LINGUISTIC** learning and **INTERPERSONAL** learning as they create a modern-day story using a story grid.

 **LOGICAL/MATHEMATICAL** learning: Ask children to think about three things that happened since they got up this morning and write or illustrate each activity on a slip of paper (woke up, brushed teeth, showered, got dressed, ate breakfast, and so on). When this task is done, invite students to work with a partner and place the sequence of their partner's morning experience in the correct order.

 Gather children into a large group and ask for volunteers to act out a story as you read it. Ask for someone to play each part (if class size is large ask for two or three robbers). Some children will want to be the audience. Assure them that is fine. Read the parable through once and then again slowly to enable children to act out their parts.

Use the sequencing cards (pictures for young children/phrases for older children) and ask children to re-create the story in the order that it happened. Let younger children ask questions. Older children can read the text themselves for clarification.

Introduce the Story Grid. Create the grid on a chalkboard or newsprint. Ask older students to fill in all the columns with the answers to these questions: Who is the victim? What is the action? Who are the passersby? Who is the rescuer? What was the outcome? Ask for at least four responses in each column. Record the responses in the appropriate columns. Then let children choose to work individually or in small groups. Give each child or group a different color marker and let them randomly draw a line across the grid connecting all the columns. Out of this information write a modern-day rendition of the parable of the Good Samaritan based on the responses selected from each column.

If time allows, share the stories, post them in your room, have them printed in the church newsletter, or create a bulletin board.

 *Musical/Rhythmic:* Have children write words to a familiar song to tell the story.

Visual/Spatial: Have children make puppets and perform the story for a younger class.

71

Intrapersonal: Have students think about when:

- They have been the robber—robbing someone of their self-esteem or dignity by put-downs and exclusion.
- They have crossed to the other side—avoiding someone who really needed a friend; perhaps the class nerd or an aging relative.
- They have been the good neighbor by helping someone who is in need— maybe helping someone with chores, or a friend with his homework.

 **LESSON EVALUATION** See form on page 98.

LESSON 20

THE LOST SHEEP

 **SCRIPTURE**   Luke 15:1-7

 **LESSON FOCUS**   God celebrates when the lost is found.

 **INTELLIGENCE FOCUS**   INTERPERSONAL
Verbal/Linguistic
Visual/Spatial

 **MATERIALS**

- [ ] patterns for sheep/ shepherd/shepherd's crook
- [ ] markers
- [ ] yarn
- [ ] tree branch for each student
- [ ] paper/pencils
- [ ] paper towel tubes
- [ ] newsprint/markers

 **LEARNING AREA**

- [ ] space to search for "lost" objects
- [ ] table for artwork and writing

 **LEARNING PROCESS**

INTERPERSONAL learning connects with VERBAL/LINGUISTIC learning as children share feelings about a time when

73

they have been lost and connect those feelings with the parable. **VISUAL/SPA-TIAL** learning and **BODY/KINESTHETIC** learning connect as children manipulate the figures, the twig, and the yarn to create a stabile about the story.

INTERPERSONAL learning: As children enter your room, tell them you have lost something you value (book, purse, keys, and so on). Ask them to help you find it. When a child finds your object, express joy and thankfulness. Tell the children that for the next three lessons they will be learning about things that have been lost and found. They will talk about a lost sheep, a lost coin, and a lost son. Tell them they will look for things that are the same in each of these stories and what Jesus is teaching them about God through these three stories.

Then invite children to form groups of three or four and share with one another about a time they had been lost (or know about someone who had been lost). Ask them to tell in as much detail as possible about the experience and mention the feelings of both themselves and the persons who were with them. Ask them to talk about how it happened and how it felt when they were found.

Gather children together and invite someone to read Luke 15:1-7. Ask them to consider how their story about being lost and Luke's story about the lost sheep are similar. Create a concept map (page 102) with the word *LOST* in a circle in the center. Add to the paper images that express the feelings associated with being lost.

Using the patterns provided, the younger children can color the pictures and hang them with yarn from the tree branch, older students can weave a pattern with the yarn around the branches of the twig incorporating the characters into the weaving. Remind them of the expression that would be on the shepherd's face. Ask them to think of the story as they create their stabile.

Display this artwork in your room or in the hallway.

Tell students that in the next lesson they will hear another story about a coin that was lost. Ask them to bring a special coin with them (perhaps from the tooth fairy/a collection/a foreign country) and to put their name on the back with tape. Send notes with this information home to parents of younger children.

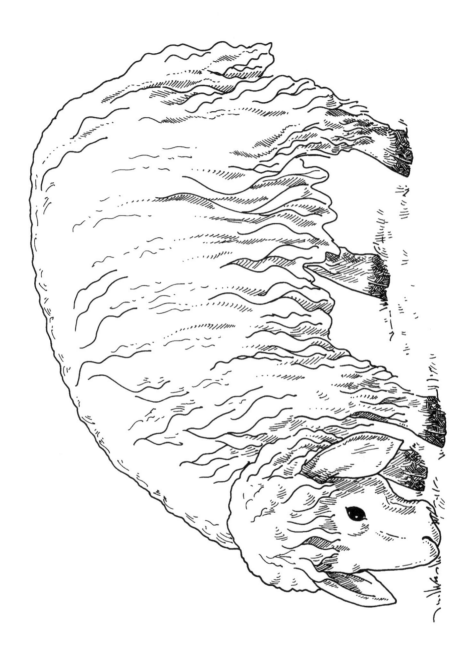

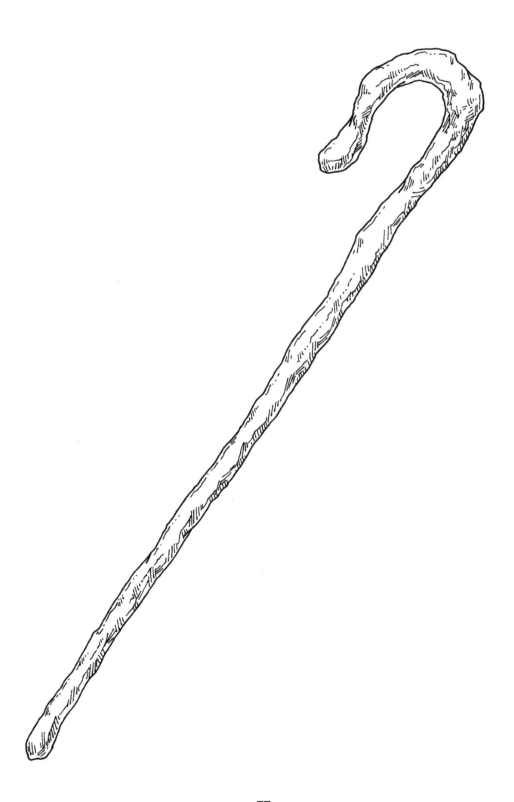

 **VARIATIONS** *Logical/Mathematical:* Older children can create a word search using words from the story on a large lined piece of newsprint, butcher paper, or the back of a grocery bag. Younger children can find objects hidden in the room.

Musical/Rhythmic: Shepherds often played a flutelike instrument to calm their sheep. Have the children create such an instrument out of a paper towel roll. They can punch holes or color holes in it to make it resemble an instrument. Ask them what kinds of music might be best to calm down the sheep. They can pretend to play a soothing song to calm the sheep.

Intrapersonal: Have students reflect on the life of a shepherd. Most often shepherds were alone for weeks with no company other than their sheep. Their sense of duty was strong because each shepherd knew that all these animals depended on him for their safety. Have them imagine what it must be like to have been a shepherd.

 **LESSON EVALUATION** See form on page 98.

LESSON 21

THE LOST COIN

 **SCRIPTURE** Luke 15:8-10

 **LESSON FOCUS** God celebrates when the lost is found.

 **INTELLIGENCE FOCUS**

INTERPERSONAL
Logical/Mathematical
Visual/Spatial
Musical/Rhythmic
Body/Kinesthetic

 **MATERIALS**

- [ ] special coins from children
- [ ] broom
- [ ] shawl
- [ ] paper/pencil

 **LEARNING AREA**

- [ ] tables for display and writing song
- [ ] space for acting out the story

 **LEARNING PROCESS** INTERPERSONAL learning connects with LOGICAL/MATHEMATICAL learning and VISUAL/SPATIAL learning as children tell about their special coins and arrange them in a pattern. BODY/KINESTHETIC learning connects with MUSICAL/RHYTHMIC learning as children act out the story and write a song to accompany the actions.

 **WARM-UP** | **INTERPERSONAL** learning happens when children place their special coins on a table (see Lesson 20). Invite each child to talk about his or her coin and why it is special. Let the children discover patterns in the coins (size, color, dates) and talk about the many right answers they have found.

Ask them how they would feel if their special coin was lost. Ask what they would do to find it. Ask how they might feel when they found it.

 **LESSON** | Tell them that there is a story about a woman in the Bible who lost her coin. Have one of the students read the two verses. Ask if there are any questions.

Invite students to stand and act out the story as it is read again slowly. Each child can pantomime the story, expressing all the actions and emotions that are read.

Now ask children in groups of three or four to write words to a familiar song about this story. Allow ample time. Then as each group sings their song, the rest of the students act out the parts. Younger children can learn the words to this story in the form of a song to the tune of "Mary Had a Little Lamb." (See page 106.) Explain that in the next lesson they will hear yet another story about God celebrating when what has been lost is found. This time it is a young man who gets lost.

 **VARIATIONS** | *Intrapersonal* and *Verbal/Linguistic:* Have children imagine that they are the coin that has been lost. Ask: How do you feel? Are you frightened? Lonely? Hopeful? After older children have thought about how they might have felt, have them write a first-person story as the woman's coin. Put into words how it felt to be lost and found. Younger children can tell their story in a circle with one child beginning the story, and after a sentence or two have the next child take up the story. Invite lots of creative ideas about how the coin felt being lost.

 **LESSON EVALUATION** | See form on page 98.

THE PARABLE OF THE LOVING FATHER

 **SCRIPTURE**   Luke 15:11-32

 **LESSON FOCUS**   God celebrates when the lost is found.

 **INTELLIGENCE FOCUS**

INTRAPERSONAL
Interpersonal
Body/Kinesthetic
Musical/Rhythmic
Verbal/Linguistic
Logical/Mathematical
Visual/Spatial

MATERIALS

- ☐ masking tape
- ☐ paper
- ☐ pencils

LEARNING AREA

- ☐ large space so that children can move on the continuum
- ☐ space for making three large circles on the floor

 **LEARNING PROCESS**

Options for all seven ways of learning are presented as children select feelings and create a large Venn diagram of the similarities and differences of the three stories in Luke's Gospel. Ask children to make connections that will lead to self-discovery of the message that Jesus is giving through these stories. The message is so powerful, Luke includes it in three ways to help us understand.

 **WARM-UP** BODY/KINESTHETIC learning: Ask children to respond by standing up and pretending to cheer when they feel happy and slouching down and looking unhappy when they are sad as you read a story to them. You might want to practice once or twice acting out happy and sad with your body.

"There once was a boy named Johnny, who stole a piece of candy from a store because his friends dared him to do it. *(Children's response)* At first he was proud of himself and thought he was pretty cool. *(Response)* But then he remembered what the Bible said about stealing. *(Response)* He wasn't feeling so proud anymore. *(Response)* He took the candy back and told the man at the store he was sorry for taking it. *(Response)* The man at the store said, 'I'm sorry you took it, too, but it was very brave of you to bring it back.'" *(Response)*

 **LESSON** Tell the children that they are going to hear another story and they will be asked to show the characters' reactions by expressing feelings of happiness or sadness. This story is about a boy who ran away. Read or tell the parable of the loving father (Luke 15:11-32).

Ask the children to talk about the feelings of the different characters in the story by showing their happy or sad body stances. As you tell the story again, stop periodically and ask the children how they think one of the characters felt at that particular moment in the story. (Example: How do you think the father felt when his youngest son asked for his inheritance?) Ask the children to stand and use their bodies to communicate happy or sad. Ask why they chose that stance. As you continue the story, stop several times for a feelings check about different characters.

Ask the children if they recall the last two stories or parables they have learned. How is this story like the other two? Then as a culmination to the study of these three stories, ask the children to form small groups of four or more depending on class size, and talk about the three parables from Luke's Gospel. Ask them to create a three-sphere Venn diagram (see page 100) labeling the three circles: the lost sheep, the lost coin, and the lost son. Ask each group to find the differences (record in circles) and the commonalities (record in center area where the circles intertwine) of the three stories. Ask them to come to a group conclusion of what they think God's message was in those three stories.

In a large, open space make three circles of masking tape about ten feet in diameter that are separate but have a center area where the circles intertwine. See page 100 for an example of a Venn diagram. Invite students to stand in each of the circles, or the center where the circles intertwine, when attributes of the stories are mentioned (examples: they would stand in lost coin when a woman sweeping the floor to find her coin is mentioned and in the center when someone who lost something is mentioned).

Younger children can talk about why they chose to stand in each circle or in the center with the leader and each other.

Older children might enjoy the **BODY/KINESTHETIC** movement of using the large floor circles when they have completed their diagrams on paper.

When the groups are finished, invite them to display their Venn diagrams and explain what they believe God's message is to the total group.

 **VARIATIONS** While some children are working on the Venn diagram other children may choose from the following:

- Write a song or rap about this story including God's message in the three parables.
- Write other possible endings for the story of the loving father while holding true to the theme of God's celebrating the return of the lost. Read the new story endings to the class.
- Create a picture of their favorite lost and found parable. Have them tell the story of their picture.
- Gather together to hum or sing "God Loves Those Who Run Away" to the tune of "Mary Had a Little Lamb" (see page 106 for the words). Provide copies of the words for older children, or sing it through several times for younger children until they can sing along.

 **LESSON EVALUATION** See form on page 98.

LESSON 23

THE LAST SUPPER

 **SCRIPTURE** Luke 22:7-20

 **LESSON FOCUS** Jesus shares a meal in community with his friends.

 **INTELLIGENCE FOCUS**

INTERPERSONAL
Visual/Spatial
Logical/Mathematical
Body/Kinesthetic
Intrapersonal

 **MATERIALS**

- [ ] acrostic of THE LAST SUPPER (See page 17.)
- [ ] pencils
- [ ] strips of construction paper with story sequence written on them (e.g., Jesus tells Peter/John to prepare the Passover meal, Peter and John find a man with a water jar, and so on)
- [ ] juice and crackers

LEARNING AREA

- [ ] large open area for sequencing
- [ ] tables and chairs for acting out the story

 **LEARNING PROCESS** INTERPERSONAL learning connects with BODY/KINESTHETIC learning, LOGICAL/ MATHEMATICAL learning and INTRA-PERSONAL learning as children hear and "see" the story, discover the sequence, and physically act out the story.

 **WARM-UP** INTERPERSONAL learning: Ask children to imagine that they are moving. They are leaving all their friends behind. Ask them to imagine a party held the night before they move with all their closest friends. Ask them to picture this party in their minds and share with someone in the class: Who would be there? What would they eat? What would they do? What would you leave as a remembrance of you?

 **LESSON** Gather children into a large group and ask for volunteers to share how they would like to be remembered by their friends. Tell them that Jesus had a party, a meal with his friends, just before he was arrested, put on trial, and sentenced to die. Ask them to listen closely as you read the account of the Last Supper from Luke's Gospel. Ask them to listen to the story again and try to get a picture of what is happening.

Ask several children to take one of the construction paper strips with one event from the story written on it, and hold it up in front of their chest. Ask the rest of the children to physically move the students who are the story events into the correct order of the story. Make sure everyone agrees on the order. The children who are the events will then tell the story according to the event they are holding. Repeat this process allowing another group of children to be the story events.

Ask the children:

- What do you think is the most important part of that story?
- Does the story sound like anything you have experienced? Where?
- What is communion? What do we think about each time we receive communion? (We think about Jesus and the ways that he taught us to live.)

Younger children can act out the story as it is read again. They can sit around the table and share juice and crackers in an agape feast with their classmates.

Older children can write a journal page from the perspective of one of the disciples sitting at the table with Jesus, or an acrostic (see page 17) for THE LAST SUPPER. Invite students to print the words LAST SUPPER down the left-hand side of a sheet of paper. Next to each letter write a word or phrase that begins with the letter on that line, such as:

L oving friends
A ll
S haring a meal
T ogether

Musical/Rhythmic: Learning can be enhanced by inviting students to put the story together in a song or rap.

See form on page 98.

LESSON 24

THE EMPTY TOMB

 **SCRIPTURE** Mark 16:1-8

 **LESSON FOCUS** "He is not here." Jesus was raised from the dead.

 **INTELLIGENCE FOCUS**

VISUAL/SPATIAL
Verbal/Linguistic
Logical/Mathematical
Body/Kinesthetic
Interpersonal

 **MATERIALS**

- [ ] empty egg cartons
- [ ] Easter symbols (see page 110)
- [ ] colored tissue paper
- [ ] white paper
- [ ] chalkboard or newsprint

 **LEARNING AREA**

- [ ] space for a reenactment of the discovery of the empty tomb
- [ ] tables for creating a cross/butterfly
- [ ] space for playing the concentration game

 **LEARNING PROCESS**

Almost all the intelligences are engaged as children interact, tell the Easter story in their own words, create a visual symbol of Easter, play a concentration game, and greet others with the good news of the risen Christ in Russian.

 **WARM-UP** | **VISUAL/SPATIAL** learning: Talk with children about surprises.

- What does it mean to be surprised?
- When have you been surprised?
- How do you feel when you are surprised?
- How do you look when you are surprised?

 **LESSON** | Ask children to share in small groups what they know of the Easter story. Read or tell the story of Easter morning from Luke's Gospel. Ask children to think about the surprises that occurred that morning. List the surprises on a chalkboard or newsprint (e.g., the stone was gone, there were two men sitting in the tomb, Jesus was not there, and so on). Ask the children, What was the first thing the women did after leaving the tomb?

As a means of remembering the story, have the children retell the story to one another in their own words, based on the surprises they have listed, while several children act out the parts of the story. Give each child an opportunity to act out the story.

Tell the children that they will learn to say in Russian the wonderful news that Jesus was risen from the dead. On Easter morning people in Russia greet one another with the good news that Jesus is risen this way: "Christos Vos Cres," which means "Christ is risen." People respond to this greeting by saying, "Voisten Vos Cres," which means "Indeed he is risen." Practice this several times with the children. Ask them to say it to their parents and to everyone they meet this day.

Have children create a cross with a butterfly emerging from it, which will take the form of a surprise (see page 107). Do not tell the children what they are creating.

Display Easter symbols (page 110) and discuss what each of them means. Invite responses from the older children as to what they think each symbol means as it relates to the Easter story. (Example: Rooster = Jesus' prediction to Peter that he would deny knowing Jesus three times before the rooster crowed.)

For younger children, create a game of "Concentration" by placing an Easter symbol (page 110) facedown in each section of one side of an empty egg carton. Place matching symbols randomly on the other side of the egg carton sections facedown. Invite children to pick up a symbol and try to find a matching symbol in the other side of the carton. This game can be played in pairs by preparing one egg carton and two sets of symbols for each two children in your class.

Invite the children to share their Easter greeting, their cross and butterfly, and the story of Easter with everyone they meet today.

Musical/Rhythmic: Have the words CHRIST, LORD, RISEN, TODAY printed large on white construction paper. Invite four students to hold up the words and say together "Christ the Lord is risen today." Then hold up one of the words at a time and say that word with great emphasis—CHRIST the Lord is risen today, then Christ the LORD is risen today, and so on.

 **VARIATIONS**

Intrapersonal: Have children think quietly about what Easter means to them, and then say a prayer of thanksgiving for God's miracle of Easter.

 **LESSON EVALUATION**

See form on page 98.

LESSON 25

PENTECOST

 **SCRIPTURE** — Acts 2:1-4

 **LESSON FOCUS** — God is always with us, as close as the air we breathe.

 **INTELLIGENCE FOCUS**

VISUAL/SPATIAL
Musical/Rhythmic
Body/Kinesthetic
Verbal/Linguistic
Intrapersonal

MATERIALS

- ☐ red/white crepe paper
- ☐ posterboard
- ☐ ruler
- ☐ scissors
- ☐ hole punch
- ☐ red yarn
- ☐ stapler
- ☐ paper
- ☐ tape player
- ☐ cassette tape of classical music

LEARNING AREA

- ☐ tables for constructing wind socks
- ☐ space to move to music

 **LEARNING PROCESS**

VISUAL/SPATIAL learning connects with MUSICAL/RHYTHMIC learning as students create a wind sock and observe it move while they move around the room to music. **BODY/KINESTHETIC** learning connects with **VERBAL/LINGUISTIC** and **INTRAPERSONAL** learning as children learn or create a breath prayer.

VERBAL/LINGUISTIC and **BODY/KINESTHETIC** learning: Ask the children to describe the word *wind*. Ask: Have you ever seen the wind? How can you tell when the wind is blowing? Ask them to pretend they are leaves and the wind is blowing them around. First a soft gentle breeze, and then a fierce stormy wind.

Gather the children together and read or tell the story of the coming of the Holy Spirit at Pentecost from Acts 2. Ask them how they think the people gathered there might have felt.

Invite the children to create a Pentecost wind sock (see page 108). Allow ample time to complete this task. Younger children may need help.

When the Pentecost wind socks have been completed, play the tape of classical music and invite the children to hold their wind socks high in the air and move to the music. Invite them one at a time to step back and watch how the wind created by the movement of the children causes the wind socks to move. Tell them that God's Holy Spirit moves in us like the wind moves the wind socks.

Gather students around you and sit on the floor. Ask them to take as deep a breath as they can and hold it for as long as they can. Practice several ways of breathing. Ask students how they can feel their breath (blowing on their hand, feeling their lungs expand, and so on). Tell them that God's Holy Spirit is always as close to them as their own breath. God is always with them.

Teach your students a breath prayer. A breath prayer is a simple prayer of very few words that is repeated as we breathe in and out. Teach younger children to say "Dear God" as they breathe in and "be with me" as they breathe out. It may take some practice to breathe and talk at the same time. Tell them they can say this prayer anytime and anywhere and know that God is always with them. Encourage older children to create their own words to make a very personal breath prayer. The only rule is not to have more than three words as you breathe in and three words as you breathe out.

Encourage the students to hang their wind socks in the classroom as a reminder of the coming of the Holy Spirit and to practice their breath prayers. They might teach their breath prayer to their parents or brothers and sisters.

 **VARIATIONS**

Logical/Mathematical: Invite older children to find as many scripture references to breath and wind as they can by using a concordance. Ask them to compare similarities and differences.

Interpersonal: In small groups invite children to share how they know God is inside of them, just as their breath is.

 **LESSON EVALUATION**

See form on page 98.

TEACHER TRAINING SESSION

PURPOSE: To introduce teachers to the theory and practice of using multiple intelligences in their teaching/learning sessions. It is important for teachers to understand why this will be helpful in their teaching.

TIME: A two-hour block of time or a two-hour segment of a longer training session.

MATERIALS:

- ☐ peanuts in the shell (some to give out and others to snack on)
- ☐ Bibles (one per person)
- ☐ paper
- ☐ pencils
- ☐ newsprint
- ☐ markers
- ☐ timer
- ☐ copies of self report card (Handout #1)
- ☐ copies of the seven intelligences (Handout #2)
- ☐ seven slips of paper with one intelligence printed on each

LEARNING AREA: Chairs and tables placed around the walls of the room to allow for presentation space.

WARM-UP: (10 minutes) As teachers arrive give each person a peanut. Ask them to get to "know" their peanut. Ask them to share a brief story about their peanut including its name. Place all of the peanuts in the center of the floor and ask teachers to find their peanut.

Say: "Just as each peanut is unique and different, so is each student you teach. Each of them is created by God with their own set of gifts and preferences. To make sure that each of your students gets the most benefit out of the teaching/learning situation, we have to know about them and how they learn best."

INTRODUCTION: Give each teacher a self report card (Handout #1). Give them ten minutes to complete their card. Ask for reactions. Which exercises were easy and fun? Which were a stretch? What did you learn about your own comfortable means of learning?

THEORY: (15 minutes) Read carefully the information from the introduction to this book. Share with your group the essential concepts and why knowing these concepts will be helpful in their teaching/learning settings. Distribute copies of Handout #2, which gives an overview of all seven intelligences. Explain each intelligence and tell the group they have just experienced all seven intelligences in the self report card.

PRACTICE: (20 minutes) Divide the participants into seven groups. Select a scripture (perhaps one that they will be teaching soon). Have each group select a slip of paper with an intelligence. Read the scripture. Give each group about fifteen minutes to plan a strategy of how they would teach that scripture lesson to children by using the selected intelligence as a base.

PRESENTATION: (30 minutes) At the end of the fifteen minutes of presentation, invite each group to present their lesson in any way they choose to the total group in a three-minute presentation. (Encourage creative thoughts and participation.)

FEEDBACK: (10 minutes) After the presentations, ask for feedback on what they have learned and how this will enhance their teaching/learning experiences.

PLANNING: (20 minutes) Allow time to work in groups to plan their first one or two lessons in detail using curriculum or lessons from this book. Have them check with one another about being inclusive of as many intelligences as possible in each lesson.

PRAY: (5 minutes) Close with a prayer about God giving each of us a unique and wonderful personality. Say: It is our job to provide the best possible means of communicating God's Word to our students. Teaching God's children is a very important ministry.

SELF REPORT CARD

- Write a short paragraph asking Jesus a question about something you've always wanted to know.

- Draw a symbol of your faith.

- Multiply the number of books in the Bible by the number of Gospels. Divide your answer by the number represented by the Trinity and subtract the number of chapters in Mark's Gospel. Divide your answer by the original number of Jesus' disciples. Write your answer here.

- Write the name of a hymn that expresses your faith.

- Depict with your body the mood expressed by one of the persons present at the Nativity.

- Name and reflect on a biblical character who parallels your life.

- Find two others who are finished and share your answers in a group.

THE SEVEN INTELLIGENCES

VERBAL/LINGUISTIC: Words and language, both written and spoken

reading	writing	creative writing	speaking
debate	poetry	storytelling	jokes limericks

LOGICAL/MATHEMATICAL: Scientific thinking, numbers, abstract patterns of thinking, reasoning

outlining	problem solving	sequencing	calculations
games	abstract formulas	patterns	deciphering codes

VISUAL/SPATIAL: Sense of sight, ability to visualize objects and create mental images

drawing	patterns/designs	color schemes	painting
pictures	mind-mapping	visualization	maps
sculptures	pretending	guided imagery	graphs

BODY/KINESTHETIC: Physical movement, knowing wisdom of the body, manipulation of objects

dancing	role-play	physical movement	miming
sports	body language	physical gestures	signing

MUSICAL/RHYTHMIC: Using music in any form, patterns of rhythm

sounds/tones	musical composition	environmental	sounds
singing	playing instruments	musical	performance

INTERPERSONAL: Person-to-person communication, cooperative learning

cooperative learning	collaboration skills	empathy
group projects	intuiting feelings	division of labor

INTRAPERSONAL: Inner states of being, self-reflection, awareness of spiritual realities

silent reflection	meditation	thinking strategies
centering	focusing	concentration
feeling responses	inward journey	emotional processing

IDENTIFYING INTELLIGENCE PREFERENCE

Intelligence: _____

NAMES	☺	☹

LESSON EVALUATION

1. WHAT THINGS WENT WELL?

_____

_____

_____

_____

2. WHAT THINGS WOULD YOU DO DIFFERENTLY?

_____

_____

_____

_____

3. LIST IDEAS FOR USING OTHER INTELLIGENCES:

_____

_____

_____

_____

STUDENTS' NEEDS:	TEACHER'S NEEDS:

WRITE A CINQUAIN POEM

A cinquain poem is a five-line poem that does not rhyme. This poem describes a person, an idea, or a thing. Cinquain poems follow a special pattern.

Line 1: The title or subject of the poem (one word)
Line 2: Descriptive words about the subject (two words)
Line 3: Action words or a phrase about the subject (three words)
Line 4: Words that tell how you feel about the subject (four words)
Line 5: A word that renames (synonym) the subject (one word)

Here is a sample of a cinquain poem:

GOD
LOVING CREATOR
CARING FOR PERSONS
ALWAYS WILLING TO FORGIVE
LOVE

Write your own cinquain poem.

_____

_____ _____

_____ _____ _____

_____ _____ _____ _____

_____

VENN DIAGRAM

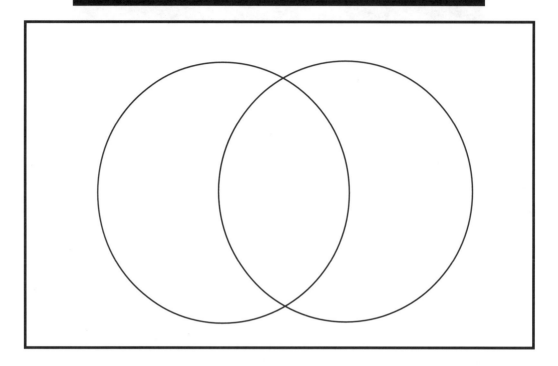

VENN DIAGRAM (example)

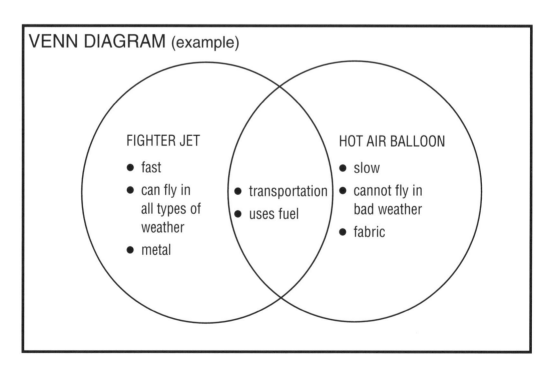

FIGHTER JET
- fast
- can fly in all types of weather
- metal

- transportation
- uses fuel

HOT AIR BALLOON
- slow
- cannot fly in bad weather
- fabric

STORY GRID (example)

GOOD GUY	SIDEKICK	BAD GUY	GAL	CONFLICT	SETTING	ENDING
doctor	small boy	city slicker	lawyer	man vs. nature	1800s	cliff-hanger
lawyer	farmer	land baron	gambler	ranchers vs. farmers	closet	everyone happy
Indian chief	deputy	bully	school-teacher	town vs. stranger	Montana	serial
marshall	relative	ex-con	widow	large bank deposit lost	town	tragic
stranger	friend	gambler	little kid	man vs. self	desert	butler did it
bar-tender	a dog	politician	Eastern cousin	good vs. evil	saloon	bad guy wins
shop owner	rancher	lawyer	bank clerk	cowboys vs. Indians	mountain	everyone dies

CONCEPT MAP

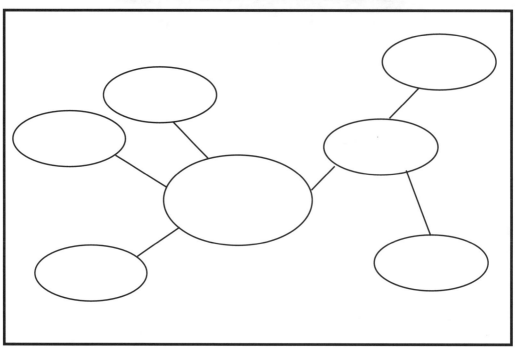

CONCEPT MAP (example)

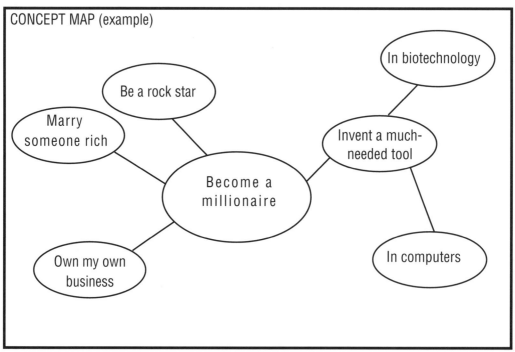

SEE/FEEL T-CHART

Object _____

WHAT I SEE	HOW I FEEL

Write two sentences:

1. Things our team saw in the object are _____

_____

2. My feelings about the object are _____

_____

WHAT, SO WHAT, NOW WHAT?

WHAT? (What did I learn from this story?)

SO WHAT? (What difference does it make now that I know this?)

NOW WHAT? (How can I use this information to make a difference in my life?)

WHAT?	SO WHAT?	NOW WHAT?

SONGS

GOD'S FRIEND NOAH

(Tune of "Old MacDonald"—Lesson 2)

God's friend Noah built an ark, *alle-alle-lu*

And on that ark he took two lions, *alle-alle-lu*

With a **roar roar** here, a **roar roar** there,

Here a **roar**, there a **roar**, everywhere a **roar**, **roar**

God's friend Noah built an ark, *alle-alle-lu*.

Invite the children to suggest animals and sounds.

JESUS HEALED HIM

(Tune of "Jesus Loves Me"—Lesson 18)

Jesus healed him this we know,
For the Bible tells us so;
Friends brought a sick man to him,
Jesus freed him of his sin.
Yes, Jesus healed him, Yes, Jesus healed him,
Yes, Jesus healed him, the Bible tells us so.

Friends let him down through the roof,
Of Jesus' power they had proof;
People questioned what he'd do,
Jesus healed him through and through.
Yes, Jesus healed him,
Yes, Jesus healed him,
Yes, Jesus healed him, the Bible tells us so.

A WOMAN LOST A LITTLE COIN

(Tune of "Mary Had a Little Lamb"—Lesson 21)

A woman lost a little coin, little coin, little coin,
A woman lost a little coin, and it was hard to find.

Looking hard she swept her house, swept her house, swept her house,
Looking hard she swept her house, and there she found the coin.

Now the woman sang with joy, sang with joy, sang with joy,
Now the woman sang with joy, and called her friends to party.

GOD LOVES THOSE WHO RUN AWAY

(Tune of "Mary Had a Little Lamb"—Lesson 21)

If I ran away today, away today, away today,
If I ran away today, could I still come home?

If you ran away today, away today,
away today,
If you ran away today, you could
still come home.

God loves those who run away, run away, run
away,
God loves those who run away, and cheers when they come home.

BUTTERFLY/CROSS

Cut a slit in the center of the cross. Take a sheet of colored tissue paper 5" x 7" and fold it in half. Cut the edges to resemble a butterfly's wings. Fold the butterfly accordion style in one-inch folds. While it is folded, insert it into the slot in the cross. Carefully open the tissue paper to form a butterfly emerging from the center of the cross. If there is time invite the children to decorate the butterfly before folding it.

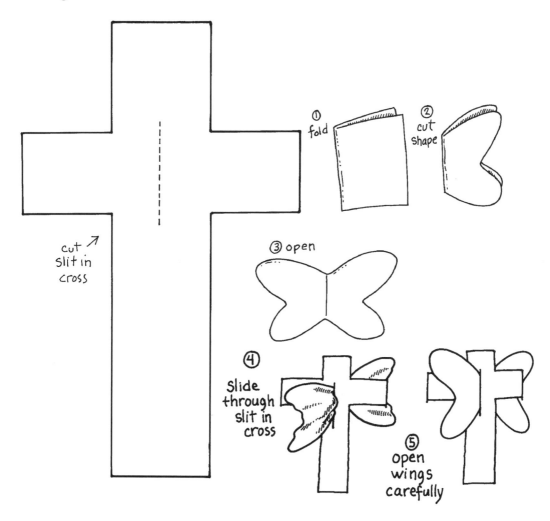

PENTECOST WIND SOCK

1. Cut a strip of posterboard two inches wide and ten inches long.
2. Decorate the strip by writing the word *Pentecost* in red marker all the way around.
3. Punch three holes equally spaced around the top of the strip.
4. Cut three pieces of red or white yarn twelve inches long.
5. Tie one piece of yarn through each hole and knot it.
6. Gather the three pieces of yarn at the other ends and tie them together in a knot.
7. Cut streamers of red and white crepe paper eighteen inches long.
8. Staple the strips of crepe paper along the bottom of the posterboard strip.
9. Staple the posterboard strip at the ends to form a ring.

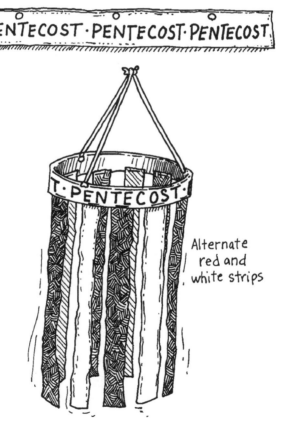

Alternate red and white strips

THE TEN COMMANDMENTS

1. You shall have no other gods before me.

2. You shall not make for yourself an idol in the form of anything in heaven above or on the earth beneath or in the waters below. You shall not bow down to them or worship them; for I, the LORD your God, am a jealous God, punishing the children for the sin of the fathers to the third and fourth generation of those who hate me, but showing love to a thousand generations, of those who love me and keep my commandments.

3. You shall not misuse the name of the LORD your God, for the LORD will not hold anyone guiltless who misuses his name.

4. Remember the Sabbath day by keeping it holy.

5. Honor your father and your mother, so that you may live long in the land the LORD your God is giving you.

6. You shall not murder.

7. You shall not commit adultery.

8. You shall not steal.

9. You shall not give false testimony against your neighbor.

10. You shall not covet your neighbor's house. You shall not covet your neighbor's wife, or his manservant or maidservant, his ox or donkey, or anything that belongs to your neighbor.

(Exodus 20:3-17 NIV)

EASTER SYMBOLS

JUDAS BETRAYED JESUS FOR THIS.

THESE WERE WAVED AS JESUS ENTERED JERUSALEM.

SOLDIERS USED THESE TO GAMBLE FOR JESUS' CLOTHES.

JESUS TOLD PETER BEFORE THE ROOSTER CROWED, HE WOULD DENY HIM THREE TIMES.

THIS WAS TO MOCK JESUS AS KING OF THE JEWS.

USED TO HOLD JESUS ON THE CROSS.

SYMBOL OF NEW LIFE.

WE REMEMBER JESUS WHEN WE CELEBRATE COMMUNION.

PILOT WASHED HIS HANDS OF JESUS' DEATH.

BIBLIOGRAPHY

Chapman, Carolyn. *If the Shoe Fits: How to Develop Multiple Intelligence in the Classroom.* Palatine, Ill.: Skylight Publishing, 1993.

Gardner, Howard. *Frames of Mind: The Theory of Multiple Intelligences.* New York: Basic Books, 1983.

Lazear, David. *Seven Ways of Knowing: Teaching for Multiple Intelligences.* Palatine, Ill.: Skylight Publishing, 1991.

_____. *Seven Ways of Teaching: The Artistry of Teaching for Multiple Intelligences.* Palatine, Ill.: Skylight Publishing, 1991.

Wycoff, Joyce. *Mindmapping: Your Personal Guide to Exploring Creativity and Problem Solving.* New York: Berkeley Books, 1991.